CREATIVE
PATCHWORK
A Practical Guide

CREATIVE PATCHWORK

A Practical Guide

ANNETTE CLAXTON

NH

NEW
HOLLAND

This book is dedicated to Robert – my other half

First published in the UK in 1993 by
New Holland (Publishers) Ltd
37 Connaught Street, London W2 2AZ

ISBN 1 85368 260 8 (hbk)
ISBN 1 85368 285 3 (pbk)

Creative Editor Jan Eaton
Assistant Editor Sue Thraves
Art Director Jane Forster
Special Photography Steve Tanner
Illustrations Stephen Dew and Terry Evans
Typeset by Ace Filmsetting Ltd, Frome, Somerset
Reproduction by Global Colour, Malaysia
Printed and bound in Singapore by Tien Wah Press (Pte) Ltd

CONTENTS

Practical Projects

Equipment And Techniques

Foreword

The purpose of this book is two-fold – it is intended to give both creative inspiration and practical help to beginners in the crafts of patchwork, quilting and appliqué, as well as inspire the more experienced needle practitioner. The collection of exciting contemporary quilts will fire the imagination and get the creative juices flowing, while the varied projects have clear, easy-to-follow instructions and will help to extend skills at all levels of experience. The book also contains a wealth of basic information which will be useful to everyone interested in these three needlework techniques.

The sections in the book are arranged in the following way: Chapter One is an introduction to the crafts of patchwork, quilting and appliqué, setting the techniques in both a historical and contemporary context. Chapter Two guides you through the process of putting your ideas into practice, including finding a starting point for a project, choosing suitable fabrics and colour schemes, planning and cutting. This chapter contains a wealth of inspirational material and it is illustrated with stunning colour photographs of some of the finest examples of quiltmaking around today.

Chapter Three concentrates on practical projects, complete with step-by-step instructions. Many of the projects such as the playmat appliquéd with simple animal shapes (page 118) and the quilted cushion cover (page 122) are suitable for beginners, while quilts such as 'One O'Clock Jump' (page 114) and 'Huge Curves' (page 100) will challenge stitchers who have more experience. Practical skills including choosing equipment, working stitches and techniques, are described and illustrated in Chapter Four. The designs are so versatile that they can be used in other projects, for example Celtic appliqué (page 79) Italian quilting (page 46), and any of the log cabin arrangements described on page 110.

There are many different methods for working a technique, and if you are comfortable using another way successfully, don't feel that the one you are using is wrong. There is no wrong way – just another way of achieving the same end. However, keep an open mind, observe how others are working and be prepared to learn new tricks.

Golden rules are really common sense: Be accurate and consistent. New project, new needle. Read right through the instructions before you start making a project. Follow either metric or imperial measurements and don't try to mix them.

When you are sitting quilting, use a footstool to support your legs, whether working at a frame or on a table. Be sure you have a good light, preferably with a daylight bulb, and remember that clip-on spotlights are useful. Don't sit for hours, but take frequent breaks by walking around the house or the garden. Straighten your back by lying on the floor. Ask your doctor for some neck exercises to do before you start and from time to time during stitching.

Working at a trestle table with a top made from a door and adjustable legs makes marking up and tacking quilts less backbreaking than working at a standard height table or working on the floor. Some table legs can be raised by slotting into drainpipe lengths cut to the right size.

Always sign your quilt with your name, the quilt's name and the date. This information can be part of the creative process, perhaps incorporating the information into the design by embroidering the words on the front border, on a block or during quilting. Alternatively, attach a fabric label to the back of the quilt with the information written in indelible ink, typed, hand or machine embroidered or perhaps make the label into a miniature block. Quilt labels can also contain more information, such as a poem, a dedication to the recipient, the tale of the design and its making. Often, the back of a quilt can be as exciting as the front! This process always seems like the last straw, but provides an invaluable record of contemporary quilters for the future.

Liberty fabrics feature here as a glorious collection of flowers in different designs in tones of blue and tan worked in a variety of log cabin blocks. Liberty lawn is a fine one hundred percent cotton with a dense weave which makes it a delight to hand quilt. Liberty lawn designs are usually harmonious collections of flowers, although contemporary prints also feature in the range. Many of the designs have been in and out of production for years, so it is quite possible to recognise a childhood dress. This detail is from the full size quilt by Alison Kirkby on page 33.

Introduction

I have loved sewing since I was a child and over the years I have made dolls' clothes, my own clothes, practised various textile crafts such as soft toys and leather jewellery and eventually dressed my children in what, with hindsight, were undoubtedly some rather dubious creations.

My first introduction to patchwork was during the early Seventies when we were waiting to sell our house. I needed an occupation to keep my mind and hands busy, so I made a scrap quilt out of small squares of assorted fabric. Knowing nothing about the practicalities of choosing suitable fabric, seam allowances, wadding and backing, the quilt was shaped like a huge pillowcase which I turned through, closing the opening with a row of machine stitching! Fired by this not altogether unsuccessful experience, I decided to have a go at making another, this time using scraps of velvet. That quilt promptly fell apart and I decided that it was time to learn how to sew properly.

I enrolled on a four-year, part-time course in fashion. Without my quite realizing it, patched, quilted and appliquéd details began to appear on the clothes I was designing. A gift of some dupion silk from a friend led to the making of a machine-quilted coat. Again, I was rather hazy about the technical details of quilting but, in spite of my inexperience, the coat looked good. By this time, I was nearly hooked – but not quite. The opportunity to teach quilting on clothing led to further study of the subject and, together with my awakening interest in twentieth century art, my life took on a new direction.

My views on quilting are passionate. A feeling of deep calm or great delight can come over me as I view a quilt. The colours, the juxtaposition of shapes and pattern, even the gulleys made by the rows of quilting stitches all affect me deeply. I know that many people look at quilts and react by saying that they could never do such work, but I always feel inspired and uplifted and I long to start work on a new project.

THE WORKROOM

Now that both my daughters have left home, I am fortunate enough to have two workrooms on the same floor. One workroom is small, situated at the back of the house, and it overlooks a south-west facing garden. This room gets the afternoon sun and I use this room mainly for stitching, with my sewing machine set up facing the window and the ironing board close at hand. This room also houses my fancy materials: beads and sequins, lace, fabric paints, ribbon and braid, as well as a large collection of inspirational books. My second workroom is much larger and it receives the morning light. In the late afternoon and evening, the artificial light is good, supplied by a series of clamp spotlights. This room accommodates a large worktable, my fabric collection, practical books, floor-standing quilting frame, drawing board and a plan chest filled with paper and card. This is where I design and quilt, as well as typing letters and making numerous phone calls. My worktable is a flexible arrangement consisting of three sets of adjustable trestle legs topped with varnished hardwood doors. When the three sets of legs are placed together, the doors make a work surface large enough to take a full-size quilt when tacking. The doors and legs can be easily moved round to make a desk and a cutting-out table. It is important to have work surfaces at the right height – mine are 84cm (33in) high which means I can work at them standing up without getting backache from bending.

IN A SPIN by Annette Claxton and Jenni Dobson
141 cm square (56 in square)

Inspired by a birthday visit to St Marks in Venice,
Annette Claxton's design for 'In a Spin' reflects the
geometric designs from the cathedral's marble floors
which she thinks are "an absolute gift to quiltmakers".
The basic design was of a circle held within a square,
then the idea developed so the curved shapes spin out

and disappear beneath the next, larger curve. The
colours are very light in the centre and gradually
become darker, so that they also appear to spin
towards the viewer with the ends moving out
of the frame.
One hundred percent silk fabric, designed and
machine pieced by Annette Claxton, hand quilted
by Jenni Dobson.

THE QUILTING PROCESS

It usually takes me about three months to complete one of my quilted pieces. The processes are demanding but each is enjoyable in its own way. When designing a new project, I don't allow myself to think about how the quilt will be constructed, as this can restrict creativity. I sit in my second workroom surrounded by piles of fabric pieces, glancing at them from time to time. I then mark out lots of 10cm (4in) squares on graph paper and begin to fill them with different designs and variations. When one square appears to work visually, I enlarge the design to

GOING INTO COLOUR
by Annette Claxton
130 cm square (51 in square)
The design was inspired by Art Deco architecture of the Thirties and Annette Claxton's admiration for the artists Sonia and Robert Delaunay.

twice the size and look at its possibilities more carefully, sometimes adding colour. I often do this several times until I am happy with a design.

The next stage is to draw up my final design to full size on dressmaker's pattern paper, a process known as drafting. Once the design is drafted, I make a final selection of fabrics and take endless trouble to obtain just the right colour. I always try to work logically, gradually patching and pinning the results on to my softboard wall. This is a wall in my second workroom which is covered with pieces of soft insulating board from a DIY store. The insulating board is painted white. Designs, fabric swatches and pieces of work in progress are pinned securely to the softboard wall, so I can stand back and gauge the effect of my efforts.

When a quilt top is complete, it is laid over a piece of wadding and a suitable backing fabric, then the three layers are tacked together. I enjoy tacking – the rhythm of the stitching is calming and I feel that the quilt is under control. The actual quilting progresses gradually as it's such a slow process, but friends can pop in and chat, or I can listen to the radio and spend time thinking.

When a quilt is finished, I tend to feel quite detached for a while. I need to go to exhibitions, clean the house, visit friends, or tidy the garden before the whole process can start again. I am then happy to live with my finished quilt as I feel it has become part of my family. On average, I make three quilts per year and they are all for sale, unless made specially for my family. I have several on display at home at any one time, usually hanging on walls, with the remainder carefully rolled in acid-free tissue paper clearly labelled and stored in white cotton sheets.

THE VARIOUS TECHNIQUES

Patchwork, quilting and appliqué are three distinct techniques, all of which may be used alone or combined with each other. The term patchwork describes the art of joining coloured patches of fabric together to make a larger piece with a secondary design.

Patchwork can be worked by hand or machine and although both methods require great dedication and many patient hours of work, the results are always worthwhile, whether they are traditional or original designs. The rich variety of patchwork techniques, from the straight strips of log cabin through crazy patchwork to formal repeated blocks joined together, often brings unexpected results which are enhanced by the endless possibilities of colour and tone contrasts.

FIREWORKS by
Irene MacWilliam
94 cm square (37 in square)
Irene MacWilliam's wall hanging is an original adaptation of log cabin blocks. The quilt was made for the Irish Patchwork Society's tenth Anniversary Exhibition which had the theme of celebration. The silks and cottons catch the light, giving the impression of fireworks exploding high in the night sky. One hundred percent silk and cotton fabrics, hand pieced, tie quilted with metallic threads.

Quilting is the technique which secures two or more layers of fabric together by stitching, usually with the addition of wadding or other type of filling. Quilting has been known in Europe since the Middle Ages, when its use was probably more functional than decorative. Quilted waistcoats were used as light armour to protect soldiers from glancing arrows and quilted garments were also used under armour to prevent metal from chafing delicate skin.

Appliqué is the application of a fabric motif of any sort to a background fabric and variations of this technique can be found around the world, from Europe to South America.

The three techniques can be used independently or freely combined with each other. Patchwork items are often quilted and may also include areas of decorative appliqué. Similarly, a piece of appliqué may be quilted and can also contain areas of patchwork. Quilting is the generic name for all three crafts, and this term is used to describe both clothing, bedding and wallhangings made in this way. The term 'quilter' covers the people who practice any of the three needlework skills.

All three techniques can be worked by hand or machine, depending on both the chosen design and your personal preference. The pleasures of sewing by hand, perhaps sitting quietly at home or whiling away the miles on a journey, can be weighed up against the advantages of using a sewing machine. Machining, although having the distinct benefit of speed, is usually a solitary occupation as the noise from the motor rules out conversation. The ideal situation is to have more than one project on the go at once so you can combine hand and machine work to suit your circumstances.

FLYING GEESE, (Maker Unknown) Northumberland, 1880
208 cm × 213 cm (82 in × 84 in)
This striking red and white quilt from the north of England has a beautifully dramatic design. The maker obviously had some trouble resolving the corners of the sawtooth bands! However, it is an honourable tradition in quiltmaking that a small mistake or two is quite acceptable, as only God is seen to be perfect. One hundred percent cotton, hand pieced and quilted.

THE EARLIEST PATCHWORK

Patchwork is not a new craft. Making clothing from joining animal skins must have been one of man's primary instincts. This process has been refined over the years and today, patchwork is a popular and fascinating craft which is practised by men and women from every walk of life, all over the world.

Various claims have been made regarding the dates when the first pieces of patchwork, quilting and appliqué were made, but evidence is hard to substantiate due to the fragile nature of fabric over long periods of time. One or two fragments survive from the distant past, but very little from before five or six hundred years ago. A wall painting in Thebes depicts an Egyptian sailing boat from the times of Rameses III (1198 to 1166 BC) with patched sails decorated with a striped chevron border. A quilted funerary carpet thought to be from the first century BC is in the possession of the St Petersburg Department of the Institute of Archaeology of the Academy of Sciences. The quilted designs show spirals with smaller scroll patterns, diamond cross hatching and geometric interlacing patterns. The carpet also has designs of wild beasts worked in applied thread. The earliest piece of appliqué is thought to be a ceremonial canopy made from dyed gazelle hide cut into many different patterns. The canopy dates from about 980 BC and it is housed in the Boulak Museum, Cairo.

We are, therefore, dependent on historical records such as household accounts, paintings and letters. Averil Colby in her classic book *Quilting* refers to historical references that quilted bedcovers were an accepted furnishing in many parts of Europe as early as 1290 and quotes 'Maketh a bed . . . of quoiltene (quilting) and of materasz' which indicates that the quilting was used as a covering, rather than as a mattress.

It is always interesting to visit a museum or costume collection to look at historical examples of patchwork, quilting and appliqué. These three techniques were used over the centuries for the

same reasons that we use them today – decoration, warmth, economy and creativity. Paral-
lels can be found in the clothing decoration seen
in some of the world's greatest paintings. Pictures
of aristocrats wearing sumptuous garments made
from luxurious embroidered fabrics ornamented
with jewels and lace often show that the garments
were quilted in one part or another, either in the
bodice, sleeve, skirt, petticoat or cap.

The National Portrait Gallery in London has
on display a 16th century portrait by Titian
which shows a man wearing a garment with rich
blue quilted satin sleeves. In practical terms,
quilting made the garments warmer, an important feature when living in a chilly castle or
mansion. Garments would be passed on through
the household until they were worn out, then
fragments were saved and recycled in patches of
one sort or another.

RECYCLING OLD FABRICS

One of the primary requirements of patchwork
was the need to make warm bedding by recycling
old clothes and other fabric items. Although
functional, the quilts made by American pioneer
men and women, and those from the poorer
areas of Britain during the nineteenth and
twentieth centuries, show great creativity in both
design and colour combinations. The materials
range from outgrown children's clothes, pieces of
salvaged cotton and wool fabric, hoarded scraps
of silk, satin, ribbon and velvet, to old army
uniforms and pieces of fabric from sample books.
The fillings are also diverse, varying from sheep's
wool gathered in the hedgerows, to layers of well-
worn cloth, threadbare blankets, and even old
quilts, quilted through again.

*DIAMOND IN A STAR, Amish
(Maker Unknown), 1920
190 cm × 196 cm (75 in × 77 in)
The subtle arrangement of colours
in this Amish quilt shows up the
quilting pattern beautifully and
brightly coloured binding echoes the
borders radiating from the central
diamond. The fabric is pure wool,
probably the same type of fabric
used by Amish women to make their
garments. One hundred percent
wool, hand pieced and quilted.*

The making of this type of patchwork gradually declined after the 1950s when the economies of both the USA and Britain revived after the Second World War and the policy of 'make do and mend' was considered outdated. By the late 1960s, the prevailing fashion for nostalgia in both clothing and lifestyle caused many people to look back to earlier times for inspiration, and they rediscovered and revived the simple values of the early settlers together with their rustic furniture, clothes and traditional patchwork quilts.

TRADITIONAL QUILTING AS INSPIRATION

The study of garments from 18th century Europe and earlier shows a wealth of quilting used in clothes for both men, women and children. Today, these garments are a wonderful source of design inspiration and show how fashions in decoration overlap into all forms of artistic endeavour. Designs with similar themes such as the scroll, feather, pineapple, fan, paisley motif and clamshell have been used in many different ways, from church carvings to book illustrations. Antique embroidered and brocaded floral designs are often used as print designs.

Slashing silk garments to reveal another fabric underneath was a widely used technique during the 16th century while padded quilting was used to decorate waistcoats, petticoats and headwear from the 17th century on. These techniques have survived the centuries and form part of the modern quilter's links with the past.

Decoration on clothes has always been used as a status symbol. In hot countries where clothing was scanty, images were painted on the body but decorative textiles were found in household items and ceremonial hangings.

Today, we wear our quilted clothing as a statement of our skill, creativity, resourcefulness and still, occasionally, of course, in cold climates, for warmth.

THE ORIGINS OF QUILTING

It is generally accepted that quilting was introduced to America and elsewhere by English and European settlers from around the beginning of the 17th century, but as these communities grew, various quilting techniques became popular, were developed and spread from quilter to quilter and are now associated with and named after the original makers. The Amish community of Pennsylvania were governed by strict teachings of their Church and lived their lives simply and frugally. Their homes and clothing were plain without added decoration. Amish quilts were simple in construction, but made from combinations of dark colours enlivened with startling contrasts. Today the Amish still live modestly and their quilts are greatly valued as works of art. The impact of Amish quilts with their large areas of solid colour covered with fine stitching have greatly influenced modern quilters.

Although single-colour quilts were used by the early settlers in America, it would appear that this type of quilt was less popular than in Britain. Many of the quilts made during the early 19th century in Wales and the north of England were crafted by professional quilters. Some of these were nomadic and travelled around, living with a family for the duration of the quiltmaking. There were also professional markers who transferred the quilting designs to the fabric. In some areas of Britain, quiltmakers used to leave the blue pencil marker lines so that they showed through the stitches on the finished quilt. Now we take pride in invisible marking. The quilting designs in Wales tended to be of medallion form, spreading out from a central design, while quilting in the north of England was traditionally worked in lines from top to bottom of a quilt. Traditional quilting patterns were handed down from mother to daughter, together with new designs usually copied from quilts made by friends, relatives or neighbours.

WILD GOOSE CHASE (Maker Unknown) 1910 168 cm × 172 cm (66 in × 68 in) This small, Scottish medallion quilt is a rather modest affair and was probably made for a child. The maker seems to have run out of fabric as some patches on the bottom 'Flying Goose' border do not match. The whole design has a naive, folk art quality. One hundred percent cotton, hand pieced and quilted.

THE ORIGINS OF
APPLIQUÉ

Appliqué has evolved in many cultures round the world, from the reverse appliqué techniques of South America to the beautiful pictorial designs of 18th and 19th century North America. Baltimore Album quilts take their name from the city where many of the designs originated, and they are considered now, as in the 19th century when many of them were stitched, to be some of the finest examples of appliqué ever created. Baltimore quilts were not always padded or even backed and they consisted of a number of blocks, sometimes as many as 42 in a single quilt, each

FAMILY ALBUM by Melyn Robinson
177 cm square (70 in square)
This is a modern version of a Baltimore Album quilt, with scenes depicting some of the more colourful characters from Melyn Robinson's American and English

family tree. One hundred percent cotton, hand appliquéd using freezer paper, machine quilted. (Details below and overleaf.)

featuring a different design. Many blocks had a pictorial design and portrayed patriotic motifs, buildings, flowers, wreaths and animals, but blocks with embroidered signatures, religious tests or goodwill messages were also popular. The blocks were made by friends or members of a church or community working together, and the designs often commemorated a particular local occasion such as a birth or wedding. The

quilts were presented to brides and new mothers as well as to well-loved and respected members of the community such as doctors and ministers, as a gesture of friendship. The borders of Baltimore Album quilts consisted of elaborate swags, bows, fruits and vines and the designs were flowing and bold. Complementary colours of red and green were used together to great effect. Today, they are items to be prized and

admired and the making of a modern Baltimore-style quilt is regarded as the pinnacle of achievement by many modern appliqué enthusiasts. The detailed designs are very time consuming to work and can take up to a thousand hours of work.

QUILTING IN GROUPS

The appeal of stitching together as a group has brought quilters together since the activity began. All over the world, women have drawn comfort and support from each others company while their men were absent and often this time was spent by making much-needed items for the home and family and even as a way of earning extra income. The pleasure of working on a joint project is now experienced by modern quilting groups who gather regularly to work together. The resulting quilts are made for exhibitions and competitions as well as to be given away as gifts or be donated to raise money for charities.

The numbers in today's quilting groups can range from half a dozen up to 200 men and women. When the group has a large membership, several smaller gatherings will work on their own specific projects. Workshops and speakers are organised, together with visits to exhibitions, other groups and museums to stimulate ideas. Sometimes a group will be part of a class, so the making of a joint project is intended as a learning process from start to finish.

We can see the maker's sense of fun and enjoyment in this quilt which records her family history. It shows a witch hanged at Salem, a clockmaker, a prospector, an admiral, an early American colonist, a guard at the execution of King Charles I and the shop interior belonging to Melyn's great grandfather. This detail, from Melyn Robinson's quilt illustrated on the previous pages, is beautifully worked in hand appliqué.

*COMPUTER 1 by
Neta Lewis
100 cm × 128 cm (39 in ×
50 in)
Neta Lewis's quilt was
designed with the help of
a computer, then the still
frames were captured by
photography. Two images
interacted and moved on
the computer screen and
were 'frozen' on film,
resulting in a unique
image. One hundred
percent cotton, wool
batting, machine pieced
and quilted.*

Each quilting group functions in a slightly different way. One group I visited in Australia bring all their small children to the meetings. The children play happily together, running in from time to time for reassurance and kind words. Many meetings take place in hired halls or in member's own homes. 'Show and tell' meetings where members bring in their latest works to be viewed are very valuable exchanges, demonstrating both the creative and the practical processes of the quilter's art.

My own group, Beckenham Quilters, was founded in 1980. The membership has grown to over 60 quilters who meet once a month in a large, comfortable room at a local church. A committee is now needed to mastermind all our activities and it works hard to ensure the members have a varied and interesting programme.

We have two open meetings a year when we invite a speaker to show slides and lecture on some aspect of quiltmaking. Our programme includes workshops run by members and invited guests, demonstrations, practical sessions and outings to quilt shows. Another feature are social events when we invite other quilting groups to 'show and tell' and we provide supper. In alternate years, Beckenham Quilters hold a quilt show, attracting some 400 visitors in a day. We can usually muster about 50 quilts at a show, but we also pride ourselves on the quality of our refreshments. At every meeting there are home-baked cakes to sample, so we often swap recipes as well as patchwork blocks!

Beckenham Quilters normally has three quilts in the making, and small groups meet in member's homes to work and chat. One member will

take charge of organizing the designing and making of a quilt, asking for volunteers to cut out and piece the blocks, then more help to correct any little shortcomings and join the blocks together. Others then work on the quilting and another volunteer binds the edges and makes a label and a bag for storing the quilt. The fabric is often from members' scrap bags or it may be new and paid for with group funds. Unusually, we have not given away any of our joint quilts, so our local group now has a permanent record of all its progress.

THE FASCINATION OF QUILTMAKING

Over the centuries, both men and women have been compelled to arrange fabric scraps into some sort of creative whole, while others have accidentally created visually arresting combinations of patchwork, quilting and appliqué. People from all walks of life have been attracted to the sensual delight of handling fabric, and have tried to capture this delight with fabric and thread. Everyday quilts have been used, washed, worn, recovered and finally discarded. Quilts for special occasions such as weddings, births and anniversaries have been lovingly made and carefully stored, only to be taken out from time to time and admired but not used. These traditional quilts are one of the sources from which our modern quilting ambitions spring.

Although in many ways the nature of patchwork has not changed from the days of 'make do and mend' or as a way of making the most of expensive luxury fabrics, modern quilters are utilising some of the traditional materials in new and exciting ways. Antique quilts have been discovered with paper fillings which probably made the quilts extremely warm, but paper in the form of magazine pictures, photocopies and hand-made sheets is now appearing in experimental 'art' quilts. Felt, lurex, plastic and leather, are all being used as a means of self expression. We need to look forward and embrace new ideas without losing sight of our roots.

CAPRICCIO by Dinah Travis
137 cm square (54 in square)
This piece is one of a series of wall hangings made by Dinah Travis as an experiment into building up colour and texture. She used a pink base fabric, then applied squares of brilliantly coloured silk, the edges of which were left free to fray. The arrangement of colours combines well with metallic machine thread as the different squares catch the light and appear to glow. One hundred percent cotton base fabric, one hundred percent silk squares, metallic thread, machine made.

DESIGNING A QUILT

One of the first steps towards designing and making a quilt of your own is to look at the various ways of beginning the process. In this chapter you will learn how to familiarise yourself with the various techniques by looking at and appreciating the work of other quilters; handling fabrics and getting to grips with different textures and qualities of materials from silk to polycotton; learning to understand colour and pattern; developing your own colour palette and then carrying out some simple design exercises. The chapter ends with a section guiding you through the stages of putting your design into practice, including estimating and choosing the right fabric for the job. There are photographs of quilts, both old and new, throughout this chapter to act as your guide and inspiration as you begin to develop new skills. The equipment you will need and the practical skills involved are discussed and illustrated in Chapter Four, beginning on page 137.

29

LEARNING TO LOOK AT QUILTS

Arriving at a large quilt show or exhibition can be a daunting experience for a newcomer. The colour, pattern, creative and technical expertise demonstrated by the exhibits can be overwhelming. There is, however, no finer way to learn about quilts than by looking at them closely. It's important to pace yourself when visiting a show and allow yourself plenty of time to take frequent breaks. If you can visit a show twice, so much the better. Start by looking at each exhibit from a short distance away, then move closer to look at the details, then look at the whole thing from a distance once more. It's essential to read the entry in the catalogue carefully as this usually gives details of the inspiration behind the design, materials and techniques. Never touch the quilts on show to avoid accidental damage.

A good way to start is to think about the colours which have been used and your reaction to them. Do you like the way the colours have been put together? Examine the technique or techniques carefully and judge how successful the maker has been in the interpretation. Look at the workmanship and if you feel compelled to remark on it, try to be tactful! Decide how the quilt affects you – does it make you feel calm, bored, interested, inspired? If you feel that the quilt is not to your taste, ask yourself why not. Is it the overall design or the colour, technique and finish which is spoiling its impact? You will soon find that you are able to recognise specific blocks, fabric and techniques and 'read' the quilts. It will be impossible to go through this exercise in front of every quilt in a show, and this in itself will bring about selection as you study the entries you find visually appealing. Before you leave the exhibition, go back and look again at your favourite quilts. You may like to make notes in your catalogue so you can remember which quilts impressed you. Some exhibitions allow you to photograph the entries and this can be a useful memory aid. Never copy these designs, just use them as inspiration.

Study as many books on the subject as you can, looking carefully at the illustrations. You could join a class or group to extend your skills and look forward to the day when your first full-size quilt is completed. This will probably be a block or sampler quilt which will give you the opportunity to try out different techniques. Finishing your first quilt is always a great achievement and, with luck, the finished result will be something that you are happy and proud to live with to become a family heirloom.

SATURDAY AT THE FOOTBALL by Neta Lewis
178 cm × 240 cm (70 in × 95 in)
Neta Lewis's quilt was inspired by a football match where many of the crowd wore yellow waterproofs. The geometric block design was developed from lines connecting two octagons. One hundred percent cotton, machine pieced, hand quilted.

TIJUANA BRASS by Sheila Conway
274 cm square (108 in square)
This traditional block sampler quilt takes on a whole new look with its interesting and different colour combination. Inspired by the vibrant colours of Camargue cotton which is used for the background, the quilt incorporates plain Indian cottons, patterned American cottons plus metallic fabrics made in New Mexico and purchased in San Francisco. Sheila

Conway remembers that making this quilt was a source of great pleasure as well as a wonderful opportunity to try out unusual colour combinations and new interpretations of a traditional theme. One hundred percent cotton, metallic fabrics, machine pieced, hand quilted.

EAGLE EYES (opposite) by Barbara Barber 244 cm × 297 cm (96 in × 117 in)
A wonderful striped fabric was the starting point for Barbara Barber's quilt and much of the design evolved over a six month period. One hundred percent cotton, machine pieced and quilted with extensive machine stippling.

PIAZZA by Alison Kirkby 190 cm × 198 cm (75 in × 78 in)
This hanging features an original arrangement of irregularly sized log cabin squares. The hanging was constructed to be asymmetrical but balanced. One hundred percent cotton, machine pieced, hand quilted.

UNDERSTANDING FABRIC

The fabric you choose when sewing patchwork, quilting or appliqué will depend on several things. Fabric is made from many different fibres, some natural and some synthetic, each with very different properties. Some synthetic fibres such as viscose cannot be washed for example, while some luxury natural fibres including silk need specialist cleaning. This would not matter where the fabric is to be used for a wallhanging or for a silk evening jacket, but washability is vital for a bedcover or child's quilt.

Luxury materials, such as satin, silk, lurex and velvet should be avoided by beginners. Like polyester, acetate and other woven synthetics, they are slippery, difficult to handle and mark easily with pin or needle holes. Pure silk, a natural fibre, is expensive and needs a light, confident touch as it frays easily. Lurex is often unstable and the fibres break and unravel.

However, you can incorporate small pieces of these fabrics into an appliquéd design to give you experience in handling them before you can graduate to larger projects.

Polyester and cotton mix fabric, often called polycotton, is inexpensive and readily available, but it is not always easy to work with as it has a lot of stretch. Polycotton also tends to dye unevenly as the cotton element takes the dye more readily and its non-crease properties can be a problem when sewing patchwork, which needs pressing flat after the pieces have been joined. When mixed with a pure cotton fabric, polycotton will gradually rub against adjoining pieces of cotton and cause the edges to wear.

The perfect choice is fabric made from one hundred percent cotton. It sews easily, presses flat, quilts easily, washes perfectly and comes in thousands of patterns and colours. Cotton fabric for quiltmaking comes in various widths from 76cm (30in) to 225cm (90in). The most common width is 115cm (45in). Sometimes beginners will buy a cheap fabric 'just to practise on' but this can be terribly discouraging, particularly if the fabric is especially difficult to handle and the end product is not a success.

Old wholecloth quilts were often made from cotton sateen. This has a weave similar to satin which catches and reflects light beautifully and both are ideal for an experienced quilter. Dupion silk, another beautifully reflective fabric, frays very easily so needs slightly wider seam allowances. This problem can be overcome by using a liquid fray-check before cutting out the fabric. The pile on velvet and needlecord (corduroy) reflects the light in both directions, so it can appear light or dark depending on which way it is viewed. This property can be used to great creative effect. Fabric with a direction (called a nap) demands great care when cutting out to make sure that the pieces reflect light in the correct direction. Shot silk uses two colours in its weave and both colours will show as the fabric is turned to reflect the light. Knitted fabrics such as jersey are not, on the whole, used in patchwork and quilting because of their stretchy, unstable properties. However, knitted fabric can give interesting effects in texture, particularly in appliqué and experimental work.

CHOOSING THE RIGHT FABRICS

One of the great delights shared by all quilters is choosing suitable fabrics. Hunting for unusual fabric is an absorbing occupation which can lead to 'finds' all over the world. Turkish markets, sleepy towns in the outback of Australia, tiny rooms perched perilously on top of buildings in Hong Kong and dark, cavernous shops in Portugal can be the source of surprising patterns and colour combinations. Quilters the world over are always pleased to talk about their craft and a foreign language need never be a barrier to exchanging views and enthusiasms.

Quilters tend to be 'fabricaholics', stockpiling quantities of fabric lengths, offcuts and even tiny scraps which have been begged from friends, inherited, or bought 'just in case'. When starting a new quilt, you will need to make important decisions regarding colour combinations, tone and size of prints. You will also need to consider the more technical aspects including fabric quantities, weights of wadding and types of quilting thread. All too often, alas, you will find that your stockpiled fabric pieces are not quite the right colour, not large enough, or it could even be that the patterns are not compatible.

SPECIALIST SHOPS FOR QUILTERS

The simplest solution then is to take a trip to a specialist quilters' supply shop to view the huge array of fabrics available to present-day quilters. The staff in these places are usually quilters themselves and are willing to advise and inspire beginners. Many shops also sell patchwork fabric by mail order, and will supply comprehensive fabric swatches for a small fee. The swatches are often generously sized and can even be patched into a miniature quilt. Specialist shops sell 'fat quarters' of fabric which are approximately 57cm × 50cm (24½in × 18in) and are, in fact, a metre (yard) cut in half, lengthways, which yields a strip of 25cm × 115cm (12in × 45in). Shops also sell packets of co-ordinating squares and narrow widths of fabric used for borders. Many of the specialist manufacturers produce whole ranges of complementary printed designs in a wide range of colourways. Fabric with patterned stripes which can be inserted into borders is also available and you can also purchase fabric printed with various designs which can be used in different areas of a quilt.

CALCULATING THE FABRIC REQUIRED

You will probably spend many hours trying fabrics out, holding one against the other or grouping pieces in sequence, before making your final selections. This is time well spent, as a well-made quilt will last a lifetime when properly cared for, and it may well prove to be a favourite family heirloom of future generations. It is never easy to calculate the exact amount of fabric you may require, especially for a very complicated design, so try to be flexible and always add a little bit extra to your calculations. This will allow for any errors in the cutting and piecing of the patches. Errors are not usually disastrous, as the addition of an unplanned colour into a design can often result in a lively quilt where caution might have brought about a rather dull solution. You may also wish to make changes to your selection when the actual construction gets under way, perhaps substituting a slightly brighter, paler or darker fabric or one with a different pattern in order to accentuate and 'lift' an area of your design.

As a general guide, take the measurement of the finished piece and divide it by the amount of colours you are using. Remember to add more for the seam allowance and borders which look better without a seam join. One colour may need more fabric.

POPPYFIELD II by Pat Derrick
59 cm × 94 cm (23 in × 37 in)
Pat Derrick's quilt was inspired by poppyfields near her home in Norfolk and the design is loosely based on an enlarged detail from an earlier wall hanging on the same theme. The piece is worked over papers using the English method and the quilting design evolved by working intuitively, rather than to a fixed plan. One hundred percent cotton, hand dyed, hand pieced and quilted.

A collection of fabrics piled high on open shelves looks very attractive, but in practice it is safer to store pieces of fabric in boxes with lids or in a cupboard. Fabric fades quickly and can become discoloured with household dust. When you are pulling out pieces of fabric to try them out for a new project, refold each piece in a different way before tidying them away. Fold marks are hard to remove and this is one reason for washing quilt fabric before use.

To help you track down elusive colour matches, file cotton fabric in boxes in separate colour groups. You may like to split your fabric into plains and printed ones, or keep separate boxes for unusual materials such as felt, slippery fabric, glittery fabric, velvet, net and sheers. This is a good way of organising your workspace providing you keep your 'filing' up to date and label each box! In my workroom, I have lots of boxes of fabric including one filled with small offcuts and one labelled 'razzle dazzle' which contains bright, riotously patterned cottons.

UNDERSTANDING
PATCHWORK

Every type of patchwork has its own particular charm, whether worked over paper templates in the English manner or stitched together by machine. Although most of the processes used in making patchwork consist of perfectly straight-forward sewing techniques, time will be well spent mastering the basic skills of accuracy and consistency. These are both vital skills to learn in order to produce a well-made quilt with a crisply-pieced top. The basic tools needed for patchwork are simple, and can easily be supplemented with some of the excellent modern aids now available. The quilter's ruler is a particu-

SUNSHINE AND SHADOW, Amish (Maker Unknown), 1910
198 cm × 234 cm (78 in × 92 in)
The name of this delightful quilt matches the glowing yellow and peach coloured squares surrounded by a dark blue border. The design is enhanced by small motifs worked in hand quilting. One hundred percent cotton, hand pieced and quilted.

REFRACTION by Arja Sinclair
71 cm × 94 cm (28 in × 37 in)
The colours and organza fabric in this wall panel aattempt to capture the reflections caused by the refraction of light in the facets of cut glass. Working out the design took about four weeks and over ninety hours' stitching. The design is pieced using the English method over coloured papers left in place to give depth and also to conceal seam allowances. Striped organza with metallic stripes in the weft, Canford paper, hand pieced.

larly useful tool as it will, when used with a self-healing cutting mat and rotary cutter, speed up the process of cutting straight, accurate strips and squares considerably. They both come in imperial and metric measurements.

Traditional patchwork is often the starting point and inspiration for quilters, and most successful modern quilters will pay tribute to the creativity, design skills and technical expertise of the patchworkers of the past. Although the need for warmth has given way to more decorative requirements, one fast-growing enthusiasm is for recycled quilts, made primarily from pieces of favourite dresses, inherited clothing or clothes from childhood. Recycling is no longer considered to be old-fashioned, but rather an essential part of our modern 'green' lifestyle.

Many of the most effective patchwork designs consist of repeated blocks which are made by sub-dividing a square in a variety of ways, often by folding a piece of paper over and over again. Traditionally, block designs were given names by their inventors, but often the same design will have two or three names as different quilters independently drew up the same design. Patchwork blocks were published in women's magazines in America from about 1850 and it is possible that some of these designs found their way to Britain. One of the most famous techniques to use blocks is the log cabin technique, much loved by the early American settlers. Many delightful examples of this technique have survived to the present day, using a variety of fabrics from wool to satin.

PENCILS by Joy Balley
152 cm square (60 in square)
Joy Balley developed the design for her quilt from an idea she had of using fan shapes to mimic pencil shavings. As she worked on the idea, the use of three shades of colour to give a three-dimensional effect to the pencil shapes took over and formed the final design. The border decoration is randomly laid out to reflect the colours of adjacent pencils, but by keeping lighter fabric tones on the right-hand side of the border and darker ones on the left, Joy has managed to give the impression that the pencils are contained in a box or tray. One hundred percent cotton, polycotton, machine pieced, hand quilted.

ENGLISH PATCHWORK

Newcomers often associate patchwork with the English technique. It is worked by hand, over paper templates, usually in hexagon or diamond shapes. Its main purpose is to join shapes which would not easily be joined by machine. The familiar hexagonal Grandmother's Flower Garden design is a good starting point and time spent colouring isometric paper will reveal exciting developments of the basic hexagon.

AMERICAN OR BLOCK PATCHWORK

This technique uses repeating blocks of geometric design. They can be sewn on the machine or by hand using a small running stitch. The blocks are constructed in a sequence where small pieces are joined first to make units which are then added to larger pieces. By working in a logical

SOUL MUSIC by Judy Hooworth
165 cm square (65 in square)
Developing log cabin techniques is a particularly exciting way of working, as Judy Hooworth's quilt demonstrates. The design features strips containing triangles plus cross bars of striped fabric which appear to hang in front of the squares. Striped fabric divides the quilt in a complex yet orderly way. One hundred percent cotton, machine pieced and quilted.

way, blocks can be joined into rows which are then stitched together to make the quilt top. When stitching blocks together by hand, it is usual not to sew right across from edge to edge of each piece, but to finish the stitching a seam allowance away from each raw edge. This helps eliminate seam allowance bulk. On the machine, the patches are sewn right across.

Blocks can consist of four, five, seven or nine patches or multiples of these basic numbers. The block design can form stars (Mariner's Compass), utilise household objects (Bow Tie and School House), contain curves (Drunkard's Path) or straight lines which give the illusion of curves (Storm at Sea). The blocks are joined together side by side or separated by a band known as trellis or sashing. Many of the blocks are of traditional origin and are named, but it is not difficult to design and name your own blocks. It's surprising how different the same block can look made up in alternative colours and fabrics.

CRAZY PATCHWORK

Popular during Victorian times, where they were used on tables and chair backs. Crazy patchwork uses scraps of many different fabrics which are cut at odd angles and built up over a base fabric. Embroidery and embellishments are often added, but it is not usual to quilt crazy patchwork with wadding.

SEMINOLE PATCHWORK

An American Indian technique consisting of strips of fabric which are cut and rejoined several times to create intricate patterns. It is used mainly in clothing, borders, decoration and for small items. Seminole patchwork uses a lot of fabric and large pieces can become very heavy, so it is unusual to find this technique used to make bed quilts.

FOLDED OR SOMERSET PATCHWORK

This technique is also used in small areas as a motif on bags, clothing and greetings cards. It is known as 'prairie points' when pieces are incorporated into borders and insertions or used as texture. Depending on the choice of colour and tone, a variety of effects can be achieved from the basic arrangement.

CATHEDRAL WINDOW

This is another folded method of making patchwork which joins two folded and refolded squares. A diamond formed by the folds appears when two squares are joined together, then a contrasting patch of fabric is placed within the diamond and the diagonal folds are rolled over and slipstitched in place to cover the raw edges of the patch. Cathedral window patchwork is quite complicated to work and two complete squares have to be made up before the method becomes clear and the pattern becomes obvious.

LOG CABIN

A versatile and popular technique. Each log cabin block is constructed from strips of fabric which are arranged in sequence round a small central square. The square represents the fire, the heart of the settler's home, while the surrounding strips are the logs which made up the walls of the cabin or barn. The log cabin technique looks deceptively simple, but to make up several square blocks of identical size requires tremendous accuracy in cutting and stitching.

There are a number of traditional ways to arrange the blocks, known as 'setting' the blocks, but there are also exciting modern developments (page 39, Judy Haworth) in this technique where the strips themselves are patched before the blocks are assembled. The colours and tones used determine which 'set' will be chosen to make a secondary design appear. The strips can be cut as narrow as 2cm (³/₄in) but beginners should try 4cm (1¹/₂in) wide strips. The squares can be 'set' on point, that is running diagonally across the quilt, and experienced quilters are constantly experimenting with exciting new ways to use the technique.

SAMPLER QUILTS

These quilts use a combination of patchwork and appliqué techniques, often with figurative designs. They are worked in blocks which are then joined to make the quilt top. Sampler blocks are widely used in teaching to introduce a variety of techniques. The traditional blocks give students an opportunity to practise a small example. The colours and fabrics chosen make every sampler quilt unique to its maker.

MEDALLION QUILTS

These square or rectangular quilts are very decorative and have a central motif with strips, triangles and other geometric shapes surrounding the motif.

CHARM QUILTS

This type of quilt is also popular and the quilt is made from a repeated template, usually a hexagon, square or diamond, using many different fabrics so that no two patches are alike in colour or pattern. The colours are usually arranged in a pleasing sequence by grouping patches of similar colours together in tones of light and dark. As well as being a useful way of using up any small offcuts, charm quilts also give you the opportunity to swop pieces of fabric with friends to make a really individual piece of patchwork.

NON-REPEATING PATCHWORK

This technique has one complete design over the whole quilt. It is an absorbing way to work as large areas are filled with intricate detail. These quilts are often worked out loosely on paper first, then the details are made in units, pinned to a softboard wall and changed if necessary. The final construction is done only when individual areas are complete.

COLOURWASH QUILTS

These quilts use a similar technique to the above method, sometimes with a simple square grid. Here, colour and tone give the quilts their impact as movement and depth are achieved by using fabric in a painterly manner rather as an artist would use his brush strokes.

THE PARROT QUILT by Sheila Yale
81 cm × 91 cm (32 in × 36 in)
Brightly coloured printed fabric featuring a design of parrots was Sheila Yale's inspiration for this colourful quilt. Wide strips of flower and fruit patterned fabric suggest a lush forest, while black and white patterns add welcome contrast. The use of fabric printed with animals which appear to be on the ground of the 'forest' contribute both a sense of scale and a delightfully humorous touch. Random and outline quilting emphasise movement and texture as well as pictorial details. One hundred percent cotton, machine pieced, hand quilted.

TRACKS by June Thorpe 83 cm × 120 cm (33 in × 47 in)

Animals and birds in woods near Brussels set June Thorpe thinking about this design for a quilt in honour of her first grandchild. The animal shapes came from a piece of patterned wrapping paper and the animals textured bodies were made by slashing through layers of fabric. Machine embroidery has also been used on the animals and machine tucks represent water. One hundred percent cotton, fabric dyes and paints, hand and machine appliqué, machine contour quilting.

The detail shown here emphasises the layers of fabric from this fine quilt wherever the fabric has been allowed to unravel. Embroidery thread has been used to give the quilt extra sheen in satin stitch. The quilting has been sewn in nylon thread throughout.

UNDERSTANDING QUILTING

Quilting is the stitching used to hold the wadding or other stuffing within a quilt in place. Creative quilting gives a further subtle dimension to a patchwork quilt, and although quilting to echo the patched blocks will look good, a motif or border can make it look terrific. An overall curved quilting design on straight seam blocks will give an illusion of curved patchwork, particularly using one of the blocks such as Storm at Sea where straight lines are pieced to give a curved impression. To quilt lovers, quilting is the icing on the cake, a serene sight or an exciting fresh approach.

A wholecloth quilt is made from one colour or print fabric, plus wadding and backing, which is stitched all over with a series of quilting designs. Large wholecloth quilts have lengths of fabric joined in two places to give the required size. The overall effect of a patchwork quilt can be changed by quilting in curves or other patterns, while by using different coloured threads, the colour of the blocks can be enhanced or altered. An unquilted motif surrounded by dense stitches will throw the shape into relief. Remember that a contrasting

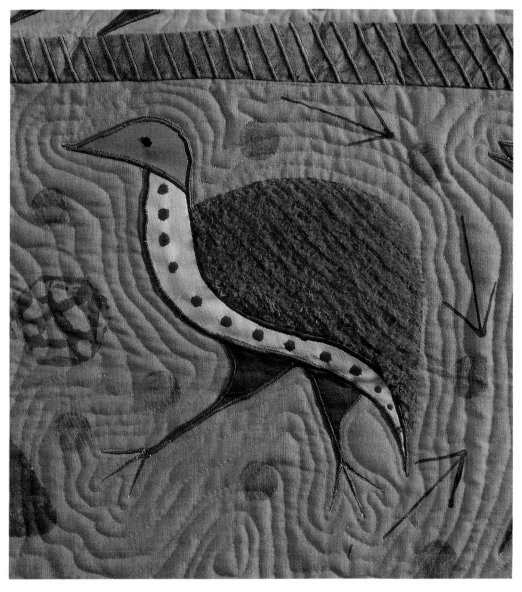

thread used on areas of plain fabric will show up your stitching, so take care to work neatly.

Depending on the type of wadding, it needs to be supported by lines of quilting at intervals from every 2.5cm (1in) for cotton wadding to every 10cm (4in) for polyester wadding. Machine quilting with its hard, continuous lines creates a different effect from hand quilting which shows as a broken line of little dashes. The decision whether to quilt by hand or machine depends to some extent on your relationship with your machine, how much time is available, the size of the piece and how you visualise the finished item. Experiment to find the most satisfactory method for you. Whatever sort of quilting you work, the quilt will shrink a little, probably by up to as much as 2.5cm (1in) across a large piece.

HAND QUILTING

This may be worked either on a frame (page 140) or directly in the hand. You will need to experiment to find the ideal method for you. The aim of quilting is to make an even run of stitches which have gone right through the layers of top fabric, wadding and backing. A between needle (which is a short needle for hand sewing) will help you to make small stitches, but if you are a beginner, start with a longer needle and work your way through a mixed packet, graduating slowly and steadily to the smaller sizes. Inexperienced quilters might also find it helpful to work on a patterned fabric with self-coloured thread while they perfect their stitching technique. As you quilt, move the needle along the thread to prevent wear in the eye.

THE PINK FISH by Pauline Burbidge
214 cm square (84 cm square)
Inspiration for Pauline Burbidge's quilt grew from various paper collage studies of a stripy still-life. The fabrics were both hand and commercially dyed, with the graded tonal areas dip-dyed to produce the shaded colours. Machine embroidery covers many areas on the quilt top, and all three layers are quilted using a multi-needle quilting machine. One hundred percent cotton, machine appliquéd, pieced and quilted.

OH! ROY by Anna Brown 126 cm × 144 cm (50 in × 57 in)
The Pop Art culture of the Sixties, especially the work of Roy Lichtenstein, influenced the design of this quilt. Anna Brown used stark, graphic images and black and white patterns enlivened with accents of bright colour which create an illusion of movement and instability. One hundred percent cotton, polycotton, machine pieced, reverse appliqué, hand quilted.

MACHINE QUILTING

Although quicker to work than hand quilting, machine quilting is not so easy to work when it comes to making large pieces. The quilt has to be rolled and held in place with bicycle clips and the sewing machine should be on a table where the weight of the quilt is supported as it passes through. A 'walking' or dual feed foot fitted to your sewing machine will help to prevent drag.

QUILT AS YOU GO

This technique is a good option for the less experienced quilter as one block at a time is patched, tacked together with wadding and backing, then quilted. It can be worked by hand or machine. When all the blocks have been quilted, they are joined together, then the backs are slip stitched together. The borders are added and the final quilting details are worked. The major advantage is that most of the quilting is worked on small manageable pieces which can easily be carried round.

MEANDER QUILTING

This type of quilting is worked on the machine and its appearance reflects its name – lines of quilting wander this way and that at random. Work meander quilting with the feed dog of your sewing machine in the down position.

QUILTING IN THE DITCH

This expression refers to lines of quilting which are worked along the gap between two seams. It is often used when the patched design is complicated and would appear muddled by more lines. The stitches hardly show and can be worked by hand or machine. It is also a good way of throwing an area into relief.

ITALIAN QUILTING

This traditional technique can use similar designs to Celtic appliqué (page 51). There are two layers instead of the three of normal quilting – a top layer in a fine fabric (often satin) and a muslin backing. The design is outlined with a double row of small running stitches which forms a series of channels. Special quilting wool is threaded through the channels from the back to create a raised design.

TRAPUNTO OR STUFFED QUILTING

Trapunto is often used with Italian quilting on two layers of fabric to create solid design areas. The shape is outlined with a single row of stitches then a small slit is made in the muslin backing and wadding is inserted into the space. The slit is then closed with herringbone stitch (page 149). Both these techniques work particularly well with fine satin and crêpe fabrics.

SHADOW QUILTING

A rather delicate technique in which a bright fabric, piece of felt or dyed fleece is covered with a fine, semi-transparent fabric and then quilted around so the colours show through in shadow form. The technique is more suited to items which will not get a lot of wear and tear. It produces pretty results used in Christening robes, cot quilts and wedding cards.

Effects can also be developed in experimental work with the insertions of sequins, shredded silk and lurex etc.

ECHO QUILTING

This can be worked by hand or machine. Multiple lines of quilting are worked to surround a motif, echoing its shape.

STIPPLE QUILTING

This technique is used in a similar way to echo quilting, but the stitches are worked at random so no clear lines are apparent. The stitches are worked densely so the resulting quilted area is quite flat, leaving the unstitched motif in relief.

CONTOUR QUILTING

This technique is similar to stipple quilting, but it is worked in lines radiating from a motif.

SASHIKO QUILTING

Traditional Japanese quilting, Sashiko uses formal Japanese designs. It is worked on two layers of fabric, often without wadding, and the stitches are larger than usual and worked in a thick thread. The effect is striking, particularly when a white design is contrasted against a completely plain, dark background.

KNOTTED QUILTING

This is also known as tied quilting and is a useful technique when working with very thick wadding. A length of thread is stitched through all the layers, then the ends are fastened in a reef knot (page 151). The knots can be made on either the right or the wrong side of the quilt and may be decorated by adding such things as buttons, beads, tassels or pompoms.

Cotton crochet or embroidery thread should be used so that the knot does not unravel and a dab of fabric glue on the knot is a wise precaution.

BLUE MOON
by Ferry Lane Quilters
157 cm × 188 cm (62 in × 74 in)
The traditional Japanese designs on the Blue Moon quilt were the result of a Sashiko workshop attended by two members of the group. The remaining members accepted a challenge to make a Sashiko-inspired quilt and sixteen members planned how the designs were to be used and stitched the quilt. Fortunately, the perfect colour of cotton sheeting was found, similar to the original blue used on old Sashiko quilts. One hundred percent mercerised crochet cotton, hand pieced and quilted.

UNDERSTANDING APPLIQUÉ

Appliqué is a decorative technique where pieces of shaped fabric are applied to a fabric background. Appliqué designs are often figurative and the applied pieces can portray a scene or landscape or tell a story as well as being purely decorative. Floral designs are also very popular. Appliqué is a versatile technique and is particularly appropriate when sewing quilts and clothing for children. Appliqué may be worked by either hand or on the sewing machine, but when worked by hand, a seam allowance must be added to each piece.

There are many traditional blocks for appliqué which can be joined together in the manner of a sampler quilt (page 31). Flowers are a particular feature in these blocks, although animals, birds, trees and baskets of fruit are also favourite motifs. These quilts generally come under the generic term of Baltimore quilts.

MACHINE APPLIQUE

There are several methods for working machine appliqué. Fusible bonding web, a relatively new material, can be used to attach the shapes firmly to the background fabric before any stitching is worked. This method gives a rather hard, flat effect so it is not suitable if the piece is intended to be quilted. Instead, use the web in narrow strips around the outline of the shape. This will secure the shape and also help the loft (page 151) when the piece is quilted. This method stands up to washing very well.

Another appliqué method is worked from the back of the fabric. The design is transferred to the wrong side, then layers of contrasting fabrics are tacked on to the right side. The design is outlined with straight stitch, then the layers are trimmed away at varying depths to reveal the colours beneath. Machine satin stitch is then worked on the front over the straight stitch lines. This technique can also be worked by hand, but all the raw edges have to be turned under and hemmed in place. A similar method is used to apply single shapes with the machine. Draw the motif on the front of the fabric to be applied, then cut it out

BIZARRE by Jane Petty 177 cm × 221 cm (70 in × 87 in)
Jane Petty's quilt was inspired by the fantastic pottery designed by Clarice Cliff, who worked in Staffordshiire, England, mainly during the 1930s. Faithful representations of actual pieces of pottery are hand appliquéd and then hand quilted. One hundred percent cotton, hand appliquéd and quilted.

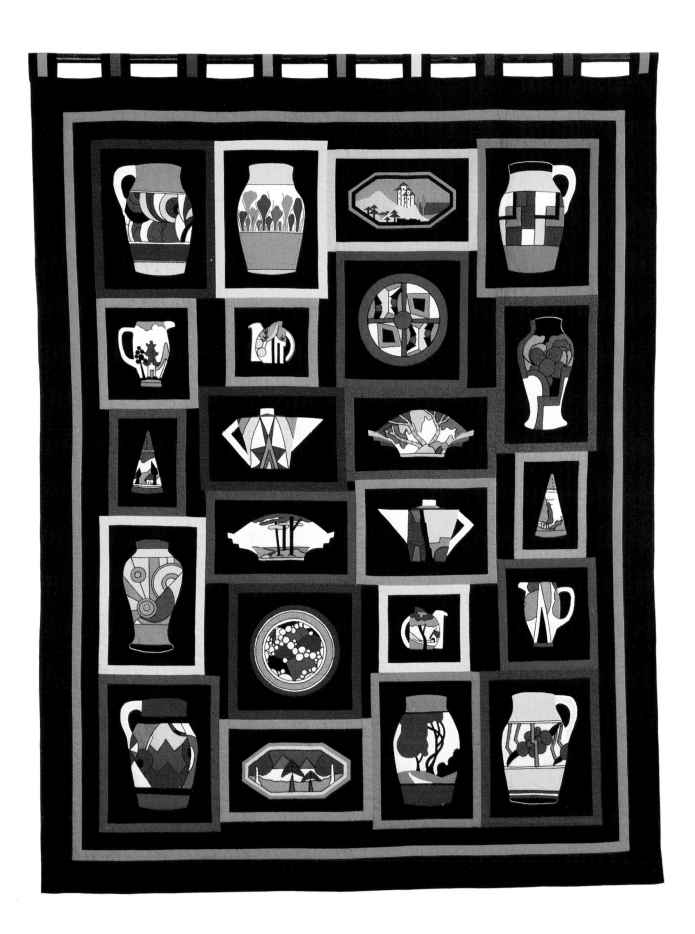

just outside the line. Stitch the shape on to the background fabric with straight stitch worked along the drawn line. Trim away the surplus fabric, then work machine satin stitch over the straight stitches.

Machine appliqué can prove tricky when the background is lightweight and it begins to pucker during the stitching. If this does happen, place a sheet of clean typing paper or a piece of stitch-and-tear embroidery backing under the work. This can be torn away after the piece is finished. Machine appliqué works particularly well when machine embroidery thread is used, but don't be tempted to use this type of thread for sewing seams as it is not very strong and will snap under pressure.

TRADITIONAL HAND APPLIQUE

The traditional way to work hand appliqué is to tack all the seam allowances under before pinning and slip stitching the shape to the fabric background. For hand appliqué, use a thread to match the motif fabric as it will blend in better than one in the background colour.

BRODERIE PERSE

Also known as Persian appliqué, this is a method of cutting out flowers from printed fabric, then applying them to the background with either slip stitch or small blanket stitches.

MOLA, SAN BLAS OR REVERSE APPLIQUE

Originally from Central America, this technique uses several layers of fabric. The layers are tacked in place under the drawn motif, then areas are trimmed away, leaving a narrow seam allowance which is tucked under with the tip of the needle and secured with slip stitch.

HAWAIIAN APPLIQUE

This technique gives a very bold effect as one large, complex motif is cut from a single piece of fabric, then applied to the background. The motif usually covers the entire centre of the quilt top. Hawaiian designs are symmetrical and are worked out on folded paper before being cut out of the fabric. The cut shape is tacked in place and applied by hand, tucking the seam allowance to the wrong side and securing the edges with slip

stitch. The curves need to be snipped so that they remain smooth. Hawaiian quilts are usually echo quilted (page 40).

CELTIC APPLIQUE

Celtic appliqué uses traditional and modern designs inspired by Celtic art. Contrasting bias strips of fabric are applied to a background fabric in lines which curve over and under with no visible joins.

FREEZER PAPER TECHNIQUE

This modern technique originates in the United States and the paper is stocked by specialist quilting shops. It has a waxy coating on one side which feels rather sticky. The paper is first cut to the shape of the motif, then laid on the wrong side of the fabric with the sticky side facing upwards. The seam allowance is pressed on to the sticky paper with the tip of an iron. The motif is then ironed on to the background fabric and slip-stitched in place. Finally, a section of background fabric is cut away and the paper eased out. This method is easy to use and gives the appliqué good loft and a crisp shape without the hardness of fusible bonding web.

STAINED GLASS APPLIQUE

This technique creates a design like a stained glass window and works particularly well with silk as well as fine cotton. The 'leading' is usually grey or black and, as in Celtic appliqué, bias strips are used. To work the technique, the pieces of 'glass' are first tacked to the background with the edges butting, then the 'leading' is applied by hand, using slip stitch worked in matching thread. It is also possible to use the fusible bonding web technique and use rows of machine satin stitch between the pieces of 'glass' to represent the 'leading'.

ALHAMBRA by Daphne Easterbrook
238 cm square (94 in square)
Daphne Easterbrook based the design for her quilt on a Moorish ceiling decoration in the Alhambra Palace in Granada, Spain, and carried it out in the traditional Moorish colours of red, blue and yellow. One hundred percent cotton, polycotton, hand pieced, appliquéd and quilted.

FREE APPLIQUE

A modern, three-dimensional technique in which pieces of fabric, buttons, and found objects are applied by hand or machine to a background fabric. Frayed fabric edges and free stitching are used to build texture as well as form. Embroidery stitches can also be included together with plastic, mirrors, chain, ribbons, feathers, felt and leather. All afford the chance to be creative.

UNDERSTANDING COLOUR

Colour affects us all in different ways and the response evoked by particular colours can be emotional, nostalgic, stimulating, depressing or happy. Colour can evoke periods in history as it has always been closely associated with fashion. We look at faded quilts, loving the soft merging of colour and tone, and perhaps forget that the materials might well have been brash and vibrant when the quilts were made. Colour has often had social overtones in Western culture, for example white implied leisure and the presence of plenty of servants to keep the clothes and household articles spotlessly clean, while bright colours were looked upon as tasteless and 'common'. This has happened on many occasions throughout history, most recently during the 1920s. Fashion colours from the immediate past always appear quaint or unappealing, but after a gap of twenty or thirty years, we are far enough distanced to view colour schemes with new eyes. Today, the bright, rather garish colours of the 1950s, 1960s and 1970s are starting to appear again, not only in interior decor and clothing but in quilts and other handmade items.

Colour influences us in different ways depending on where we live in the world. Northern light is cold and rather blue, so people living in these climes are inclined to use cool colours. The bright sunlight in southern countries tends to wash out colour visually, so vivid colours are widely used there. However, time spent in hot countries encourages us to use bright colours,

FIREWATER by Liz Heywood
152 cm × 177 cm (60 in × 70 in)
This quilt was made using the traditional block pattern 'Cupid's Dart'. The strong graphic quality of the shapes and the diagonal setting is particularly appealing. The colours were chosen to be juxtaposed so there is an element of tension at the centre of the design. It is surprising that such a 'contemporary' block design is not used more frequently. One hundred percent cotton, machine pieced, hand quilted.

LOVE IS LIKE THE WINDOW IN MY HEART III
by Leslie Morgan
198 cm × 243 cm (78 in × 96 in)
Leslie Morgan's husband, Paul, gives her a bunch of tiger lilies each year to celebrate their wedding anniversary and each year they inspire her to design from them. In this design, she has focused on the opening of the flower and the interrupted image from each flower as seen through the other blooms. One hundred percent cotton hand dyed with fibre reactive dyes, machine appliquéd and quilted with invisible thread.

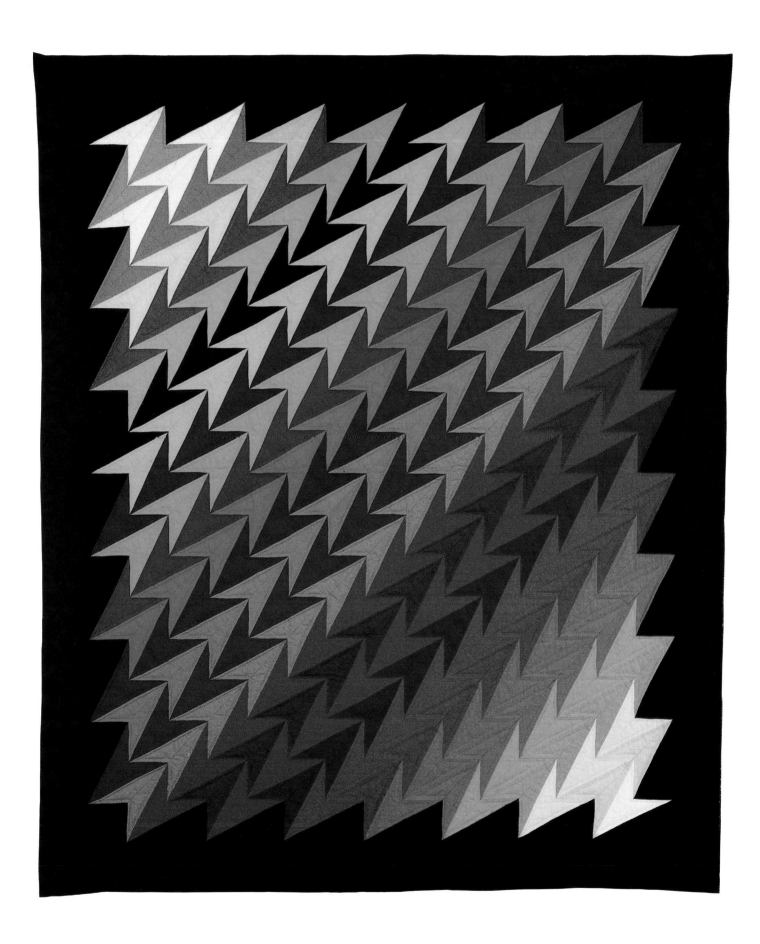

which often look even more glorious in cool surroundings than in their natural sun-filled environment. The choice of hot or cool colours depends to a great extent on mood and one can equally well choose a cool colour to contrast with bright light.

LEARNING ABOUT COLOUR

If you are not confident about colours and how to use them, spend some time following the exercises in books on the subject. Children's books on colour are excellent, describing the theory of the colour wheel in a simple way, and many books provide practical exercises for you to experiment with. Buy small tubes of paint in the primary colours of yellow, red and blue, plus white and black. By actually *making* colour you will understand so much more. Colours that are close together on the colour wheel such as yellow, orange and red share an element from either side, making them harmonious. You will also find that some colours complement each other, for example red and green, orange and blue, yellow and violet. Look again at some of the quilts you admire and see whether they fit into these combinations. Also investigate the wonderful colours to be found in nature on flower petals, birds' plumage, animal skins, insects and reptiles.

Use paints to gain a deeper understanding of colour by spending short periods of time really looking and thinking about the colours that surround you. Look at a colour wheel and try to notice how colours which are close together are harmonious and easy to live with. Observe how opposites on the colour wheel 'contrast', and if they are of a similar

strength, how they 'fight'. To learn about tones, try adding a spot of white paint to a bright colour and paint a small square, then go on adding white and painting more squares. Do the same exercise with black. Save these experiments and use them as a reminder when selecting toning fabrics for a quilt.

White and black are widely used to give colours a focus and make them appear brighter. Often, a mixture of black, white and grey shades can give a three-dimensional effect to a design, as illustrated by the Tumbling Blocks pattern. Sometimes it is difficult to see this effect with the naked eye, but holding a design up to a mirror will show it clearly. It can also be useful to photograph arrangements of blocks, as this, too, can show up unexpected secondary effects. Three-dimensional effects can be achieved by arranging colours as light (colours mixed with white), medium (colours mixed with black and white) and dark (colours mixed with black).

STARTING A SCRAP BOOK

The colours you choose for your quilt should please you but don't always play safe. It's often a good idea to venture into unfamiliar areas on the colour wheel, and if you always work in black, white, and shades of grey, try out the same design in colours. Look around your home and in your wardrobe to discover the colours with which you choose to surround yourself. Are they accidental or have you made conscious decisions? How do these colours make you feel? By giving some thought to colour and mood you should be able to come to some conclusions. Start a scrapbook or file of colour combinations which please,

*RED REFLECTIONS by
Denise Vanderlugt
150 cm square (60 in square)
In Australia, the only
stork, the Jabiru, is such
a delight to watch that it
inspired a quilt design.
One hundred percent
cotton, polycotton,
polyester knit, satin, hand
appliquéd and quilted.*

stimulate, calm or attract you. This can form the basis of your personal palette. Don't be afraid of out-dated rules such as 'never combine primaries' and 'blue and green should never be seen' but use these startling combinations for impact. Colour works, if *you* like the result! If a scrapbook seems daunting, pin up colour combinations of magazine cuttings, fabrics and postcards on a notice board and make a collage of colours, shapes and patterns.

UNDERSTANDING PATTERN

Patchwork is all about pattern. The craft is concerned with making shapes with pieces of fabric joined together, sometimes using the printed design on the fabric to add yet more

pattern, then putting several pieces together to reveal some unexpected forms. The scale at which you are working will influence the final effect. The huge lilies on Leslie Morgan's quilt (shown on page 52) are made from hand-dyed fabric machine-appliquéd onto a giant log cabin construction. The quilt is a masterly demonstration of how areas of vibrant colour can make a pattern. Her hand-dyeing technique produces a textured pattern effect.

Striped fabric can be patched or printed and will give good three-dimensional effects by changing the scale of the stripes and the angle at which they are joined. Effects such as weave, chevron and plait can be achieved easily, but stripes can also be used for dynamic or directional impact. Rotating stripes suggest movement; when they are cut into curves they will produce waves (page 132). The width of the stripes will create different effects, so experiment until you finally

BLUEBELLS II, FULL BLOOM by Susan Denton 135 cm square (53 in square) This is one of a series of three quilts celebrating the beauty of a bluebell wood from winter to spring. One hundred percent cotton, machine pieced and quilted.

manage to achieve the one you require.

We are all familiar with fabric printed with designs of small flowers and understand that, from a distance, the individual flowers will disappear into a soft blur. By using a larger scale print, the definition of each element will be stronger. It takes great confidence to handle unusual fabrics and a change of scale successfully. Dierdre Amsden's delightful quilt on page 61 illustrates this point perfectly and her individual working method utilizes both sides of printed fabrics to achieve the range of colours needed in the hundreds of small patches used.

The designs on scrap or recycled quilts (page 39), which use a riot of patterned fabrics with added embroidery, lace, buttons, beads and lengths of ribbon, are usually held together and prevented from appearing messy by the judicious use of black. Black can be introduced as a background colour, in the border or by adding 'rest' areas of plain fabric to the design. Similarly, striking designs can be achieved with checked and tartan fabrics, combined with floral prints, spots and stripes. They, too, will need a unifying colour to hold the design together in the same way as a scrap quilt.

Experimenting with fabric is a favourite pastime with many quilters. After visiting exhibitions and shops, we lay out our purchases, working out how they fit into our existing collections. Perhaps a colour block scheme will begin to take shape, followed by a quilt design

or block. There is often a shortfall of fabric, so it is a good idea to cut a small square from each piece of selected material and attach it to a card or piece of paper which can then be used as a reference point when shopping for further pieces.

APPLIQUE AS A DESIGN TOOL

Worked either by hand or with a sewing machine, appliqué can be used as a design tool by isolating areas of fabric and positioning them to build up complex shapes suggesting landscape, flowers, animals and birds. You can make a striking pattern without using any colour at all, selecting just one colour or black, white and grey. It is surprising how many tones of black, white and grey can be found in plain fabric or those with a self-coloured print. One way to judge how a pattern will appear from a distance is to screw up your eyes to look at it or to use a reducing glass, available from quilters' supply shops. This will help you to judge the effect one patterned fabric has on another.

I have always found it interesting to listen to comments at a quilt exhibition as onlookers 'see' different effects in an abstract piece of patchwork. Sometimes figurative forms will appear, including birds, faces, buildings and landscapes, which were certainly not planned by the maker. To explore patterns further, have a 'cut and stick' session, perhaps with a couple of quilting friends, cutting sections of pattern out of magazines, catalogues and greetings cards. Move the pieces around and use the designs you make as an exercise in understanding pattern.

*COLOURWASH STRIPES
AND BLUE TRIANGLES by
Deirdre Amsden
104 cm × 164 cm (41 in ×
64 in)
Myriad, multicoloured
commercial prints are
used in this quilt. Each
stripe consists of a double
row of squares graded so
they shade from dark to
light, then vice versa. One
hundred percent cotton
and cotton mix, machine
pieced, hand quilted.*

*PERSPECTIVES (opposite)
by Morley Quilters
142 cm × 203 cm (55 in ×
80 in)
The original design for
this scrap quilt by
Jennifer Hollingdale is
based on the hexagon.
Hand pieced and quilted.*

The starting point for a project can be either a piece of beautiful fabric which cries out to be used, or the desire to make up a particular design. Sometimes the two coincide. Designs cannot be worked out without some inspirational material. Scrap books are a good way to organise pictures taken from magazines, photographs and postcards, or they can be stored in cardboard files. If you are interested in a particular subject such as animals, flowers or birds, investigate the specialist magazines available at your newsagent. Design ideas can come from other media, too, so look carefully at ceramics, architecture, gardens, fish, even at pop groups and department store windows. Set aside some time to look at illustrated books of all kinds, including children's picture books, plus foreign magazines. Surround yourself with visual stimulus and let the various

influences flow – remember that designing is not a process that should be hurried.

Begin with this exercise: when an idea based on your inspirational material starts to crystallize, rule up a page of squares or rectangles about 10cm (4in) in size. This will be the shape of your final project or block. Start by drawing lines suggested by ideas from your scrapbook. The lines can be straight or curved. As you develop the idea, begin to add more detail, or if you are dissatisfied with your first sketch, move on to another square. If your ideas start to run dry, put some colour on the page. When nothing seems to be going right, draw up another page then look again at your inspirational material. You should not be copying slavishly from your inspiration, but taking some aspect such as colour, line or pattern, and developing these. Don't expect to get it right first time, but take a break and return refreshed later.

When designing a repeating block, use two mirror tiles as shown on page 139 to show you how four blocks will look when they are repeated. You may have decided to use a traditional block

*RAINBOW MAZE by
Jenny Thorburn
From point to point 274 cm
(108 in)
Jenny Thorburn's quilt
is pieced using the
English papers method
and the design was
inspired by a book of
Op-Art mazes.
Converting the maze
design into a quilt
pattern was not easy and
the process involved
careful and lengthy
drafting on graph paper.
The hand quilting is
worked in parallel lines
which follow the 'path'
of the maze and the edge
is piped using the same
black fabric as the
backing. One hundred
percent cotton, hand
pieced and quilted.*

and are uncertain what fabric or colour combination to use. Photocopy the block a few times (or trace it out) then cover the copy with a coat of spray glue. Experiment with the design by cutting out fabric to fit each patch and pressing on to the glue. Use your camera to record the arrangement, then try out more alternatives. Experiment with boldly patterned fabrics or see if the addition of an area of solid or bright colour will bring sparkle to the arrangement. Stripes can be exciting to work with, especially when combined in different widths.

When designing for appliqué, access to an overhead projector or Grant enlarger will help with enlarging a motif, but the grid method (shown on page 141) or a photocopier which enlarges can also be used. Try tracing flowers,

animals, houses and other pictorial elements from magazines, then modify the tracings by simplifying the outlines. This is a useful way of creating a design for those quilters who are not confident about their drawing skills.

QUILTING DESIGNS

Part of the design process should include the quilting design, so that the completed quilt will appear as a harmonious whole. These considerations will prevent the quilting from looking like an afterthought. When working on a design, don't assume that every part of the quilt must be filled with colour and movement. The eye needs rest space and the introduction of areas which are subtly quilted in matching thread are valuable as dramatic pauses.

FIRE OPAL by
Grania McElligott
177 cm × 183 cm (70 in ×
72 in)
The inspiration behind
Grania McElligott's
shaped wallhanging came
from a lattice-backed
dining chair designed by
Scottish architect and
designer Charles Rennie
Mackintosh. She already
had the striped silk fabric
and the lattice design
seemed to dictate the
fabric's use within a
kimono shape. One
hundred percent silk, silk
wadding and thread,
machine pieced,
hand quilted.

Looking for inspiration for wholecloth or quilting designs is not difficult. Architecture is a valuable source. Balconies, railings, fanlight windows, the carving in churches, the shape of tall buildings can all yield useful ideas. Photocopy pages from magazines as by reducing a colour picture down to tones of black and white, the main lines become easier to see. Once you become accustomed to looking for source material, ideas will probably come thick and fast! Use your camera and always carry a small notebook for scribbles. Make a note of exactly where your jottings come from, just in case they are from another quilter's original design.

THE COMPUTER AS A DESIGN TOOL
The quilt on page 100, 'Huge Curves', was designed on a computer. The computer can be an enormous help when planning a quilt. A block can be designed, then very quickly programmed to show the effect of multiple images, the design split and rotated or diagonally split and flipped

shapes can be reversed and you can see how different colours and tones would affect the design – the possibilities offered by a sophisticated computer are endless. Always seek expert advice when purchasing a computer, but you will need a Draw/Paint or Graphics programme and a print out facility. Classes in Adult Education will help you to understand your computer so you can use its facilities as an exciting and modern development in quilt design.

DESIGNING AS A GROUP

With the growth of quilting groups, many more people are taking part in group designing activities. Generally, group members take turns to organise a new undertaking and the organisation can take many forms, although traditional blocks are always popular. The 'quilt as you go' method described on page 45 is a very useful way to spread the work equally. Most group quilts are sent to the major exhibitions and the highest praise they can receive comes when visitors comment that the quilt appears to be the work of a single person.

Group designing can take many forms – sometimes a member may choose, say, two fabrics and ask the other members to make up a block of her choice by adding their own fabrics. The blocks would then be given to her to quilt and keep, and each member would have a turn to have a top made for her in this way. Challenges between groups are always fun – one group sets the other a task, perhaps specifying the exact colour, shape, inspiration or type of fabric. These challenges often seem impossible but, with ingenuity, some remarkable results can be achieved. Charm quilts (page 41), scrap quilts, and commemorative banners, and quilts bearing signatures are popular group activities.

Sheila Yale, a Beckenham Quilter, turned the making of the quilt 'All Buttoned Up' (page 65) into a game. Each member, including myself, was asked to bring a sewing kit to the meeting plus pieces of black and white fabric. We were each handed a square of calico on to which a red patch had been tacked. Our task was to sew on a second patch in black and white, finger press it, then pass the square to our neighbour to continue. The squares were passed from hand to hand until each one was filled. We all worked quickly, with much laughter as we marvelled at our neighbour's choice of fabric. The patches were then joined together and a border added. Finally, buttons from members' collections were used to hold the wadding in place.

PUTTING YOUR DESIGN INTO PRACTICE

The first step is to decide how large your project will be. When using a repeated block, aim to make your block a reasonable size so individual pieces are not too small to handle. 30cm (12in) is a popular size, but the block size must divide exactly into a size that fits your bed or cot. Borders can help to make these figures fit, if there is a shortfall, and you should also remember to add an extra measurement on the length of the bed to accommodate the pillows.

Your drafted design is the key to your quilt, so write down on it all the measurements, quantities of fabric, the number of times each template should be cut out and also attach fabric samples. Number each template according to a key. Cut your templates from plastic and mark them with the corresponding number from your key using a black waterproof marker with a fine point. When using a traditional block, write the name of the block on each template and draw on the grain line, so there will be no muddle. Make a note on either side of the template if, or when, it needs to be reversed. For curved designs, put in balance marks (page 151) along the curves. It is surprising how quickly you can forget an important detail, so the more written information you provide yourself with the better.

The previous advice is also applicable to non-repeating patchwork designs, except you will also need to enlarge your design using the grid system shown on page 141. You will not be using template plastic, but dressmakers' pattern paper, as individual sections will be large and shaped differently.

You will have read about the merits of different fabrics earlier in this chapter. The purpose of the project and the level of your experience will determine your final choice. When measuring how much fabric you will need to buy, always take into account the possibility of making a few mistakes in either the cutting out

ALL BUTTONED UP by Beckenham Quilters 183 cm × 234 cm (72 in × 92 in)
This crazy quilt was made by the Beckenham Quilters as a group project organised by Sheila Yale. The blocks were passed around the members just like a game of consequences, with each person adding another crazy patch until the calico foundation squares were covered. The squares were then assembled and the quilt top was 'tied' through by sewing on buttons. One hundred percent cotton, cotton mix, hand made and 'button' quilted.

or the piecing. When laying out the templates on the fabric, remember to leave enough space between the shapes for seam allowances. By multiplying the fabric used for each shape, you should be able to estimate the total amount you need to buy to make the patches. Add some extra to your total, it's bound to come in handy!

You may want to cut out quilt borders from one length of fabric and this will be a factor in your calculations. Cut out borders and binding strips first, slightly longer, then cut the smaller pieces. Although wholecloth quilt tops look better when the fabric is joined with seams at the sides rather then a central one, a single seam on the backing is acceptable. Add extra allowances at the sides and ends. Cut out all the pieces when you start, so if you run short there is more chance that the shop will still have some in stock.

Not all quilters wash their fabric before embarking on a quilt. However, the fold down the centre of fabric is very hard to remove unless you wash it. Dark fabrics should always be tested for colour fastness when used in quilts that will be laundered. Wash the suspect fabric and if the rinsing water continues to show colour, choose another fabric. Never use washing powders with bleach or brighteners when prewashing as these will cause the fabric to lose a lot of colour.

Whether or not you wash your pieces of fabric before you start, be sure to press them thoroughly. Fabric becomes creased in storage and will stretch when you press it during construction and this will cause inaccuracies. Start by straightening the cut edge, either by pulling a thread and cutting along the line it makes, or by tearing

RAINBOW RINGS by Jane Lloyd
144 cm square (57 in square)
Jane Lloyd's colourful design was inspired by her daughter, aged nine, who was given a photocopy of the pattern as a colouring exercise. "We agreed on the colours, I cut them out and gave them to her and in fifteen minutes she had arranged them – something which would have taken me all day – then we both added the stripes. The design is the traditional double wedding ring block." One hundred percent cotton, polycotton, machine pieced and quilted.

across the fabric from selvedge to selvedge. Snip into or cut off the selvedge as it is more tightly woven than the main body of the fabric and shrinks during washing, causing puckering.

TEMPLATES

The templates in this book do not include a seam allowance unless stated. To use a template, place it on the wrong side of the fabric, draw around the edge using a sharp HB pencil and add a seam allowance of approximately 6mm ($\frac{1}{4}$in) before cutting out. The pencilled line drawn round the template indicates the sewing line. It gives an accurate guide and can be checked easily before pressing. If a few stitches have wandered, just undo them, re-pin the fabric and stitch again. Where the seam allowance is included in a template, check the width of your sewing machine foot to be sure that it is exactly 6mm ($\frac{1}{4}$in) from the needle to the edge of the foot. The edge of the foot is used as a guide so if this measurement is incorrect, the finished blocks will be too small or too large. To correct this on your machine, measure along from the needle and place a strip of masking tape on the machine plate as a guide.

CUTTING OUT

Use sharp dressmaker's shears for cutting out any individual patches. The rotary cutter, self-healing cutting mat and quilters' ruler will all speed up the repetitive process of cutting squares, triangles and strips. Always cut standing up. Once you have mastered the rotary cutter, you will never want to rule and cut with scissors again. Remember to close the guard every time you finish cutting.

ORGANIZING THE CUT PIECES

When all the pieces are cut out, organize the way in which you intend to work and be consistent. If you have a workroom with a worktable, lay out all the pieces so that you can see that nothing is missing. Try to work in a logical way by preparing the patches so they are pinned, stitched, checked and pressed in bulk. If you use a softboard wall, use it to keep the cut pieces safe. Before you start to sew, always remember to fill the bobbin and put in a new needle.

PRACTICAL PROJECTS

This chapter includes eighteen original design ideas for quilting, patchwork and appliqué. There's something here for everyone, whether they have very basic sewing skills or are more experienced and wish to use the designs as springboards for their own creations. Modern designs and colourways have been mixed with more traditional approaches. Some projects are relatively quick to make, others will take considerable time and should be viewed as longer term propositions. To add pace and variety, there are several projects for clothes.

Small Amish Quilt

This quilt is based on the traditional Lancaster Bars pattern used by the Amish community of Pennsylvania, USA. The Amish live very simply without any twentieth century conveniences and their day-to-day lives are strictly governed by the teachings of their church. The community traces its origins back to Jakob Amman, a seventeenth century Swiss Mennonite bishop. Although the Amish dress in plain, dark clothes without any kind of ornamentation, the women of the community are renowned for their beautiful hand-made quilts. They are generally made from subdued colours of plain fabric which are then patched into simple geometric designs and extensively quilted.

Although this quilt makes an ideal beginner's patchwork project, the quilting design, which is an adaptation of the traditional feathers motif, features a considerable amount of quilting and requires a little experience. Using a rotary cutter with a quilters' ruler and a self-healing cutting mat to cut the fabric strips will speed up this process considerably.

The finished quilt measures one metre (39in) square and can be used as a childs', or lap quilt, or it could be made bigger by adding more borders or by simply enlarging the measurements.

MATERIALS

- *50cm (20in) cotton fabric 115cm (45in) wide in each of mustard, purple and pink*
- *20cm (8in) turquoise cotton fabric 115cm (45in) wide*
- *2m (2¼yd) green cotton fabric 115cm (45in) wide*
- *110cm (1¼yd) square of 60g (2oz) wadding*
- *Quilting threads*
- *Neutral sewing thread*
- *Tracing paper*
- *2.5cm (1in) masking tape*
- *Sharp HB pencil*
- *Black felt-tipped pen with a fine point*

CUTTING OUT THE STRIPS

Cut out the following shapes which all include a 6mm (¼in) seam allowance:

Mustard – four strips 102mm × 635mm (4in × 25in)

Purple – four strips 102mm × 635mm (4in × 25in)

Turquoise – four strips 64mm × 635mm (2½in × 25in)

Pink – four pieces 64mm (2½in) square
four strips 103cm × 4cm (40½in × 1½in)
four pieces 152mm (6in) square
four strips 32mm × 101mm (1¼in × 39¾in) for binding

Green – four strips 152mm × 737mm (6in × 29in)
one piece 103cm (40½in) square for backing

PIECING THE TOP

1 Lay out all the pieces following the diagram on page 72 so you can see how they fit together. Starting from the centre, pin the strips across the quilt in pairs so that you can chain piece (page 143) them together. Press the seams open at every stage. The pieced strips should measure 737mm × 635mm (29in × 25in) when pressed.

2 Join the small pink squares onto each end of the remaining two turquoise strips. Press the seams and join these strips to the top and bottom of the piece already made in step 1. Add two green strips at either side of the turquoise strips.

3 Join the large pink squares on to the remaining two green strips and stitch them to the top and bottom of the quilt. Press all the seams well on both sides of the fabric. Neatly mark the centre of the green border with a tacking stitch.

QUILTING THE TOP

1 Trace out using very fine paper the feather, oval and heart quilting designs on page 72 with the felt-tipped pen, reversing the feather design from the centre. Transfer the feather design on to the green border of the quilt (page 141) in pencil.

This quilt is just the right size to cover a childs' bed or use as a lap quilt on a chilly evening. The areas of vivid turquoise and pink fabric create a startling contrast with the sombre main colours and this effect is in keeping with many traditional Amish quilts. Amish quilts are so highly prized by collectors that many modern versions are now produced by the Amish community specifically for sale to visitors. Old, undamaged Amish quilts command very high prices whenever they appear at auction. Work methodically, piecing the centre first and then add the borders to complete the quilt top. You could make a larger version of this design by enlarging the centre square to 1m (1yd) and scaling up the size of the borders to match. When choosing an alternative colourway, remember that rich jewel colours will show off the intricately quilted designs to best advantage.

2 Rule one pencil guide line diagonally from each corner of the patched purple and mustard square. Tack the top, wadding and backing fabric together as shown on page 149. Quilt (page 147) from the centre of the quilt outwards using strips of masking tape to guide you after the first two pencil lines.

FINISHING THE QUILT

1 When all the quilting is complete, attach binding strips as shown on page 143.

2 If the quilt has been made for a child or as a gift, embroider a label with names and dates on it (page 8) and stitch it to the back.

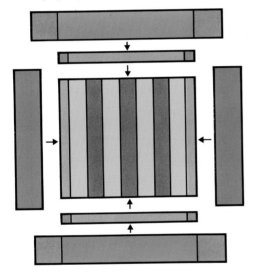

CENTRE LINE

CENTRE LINE

1 SQUARE = 8.5mm

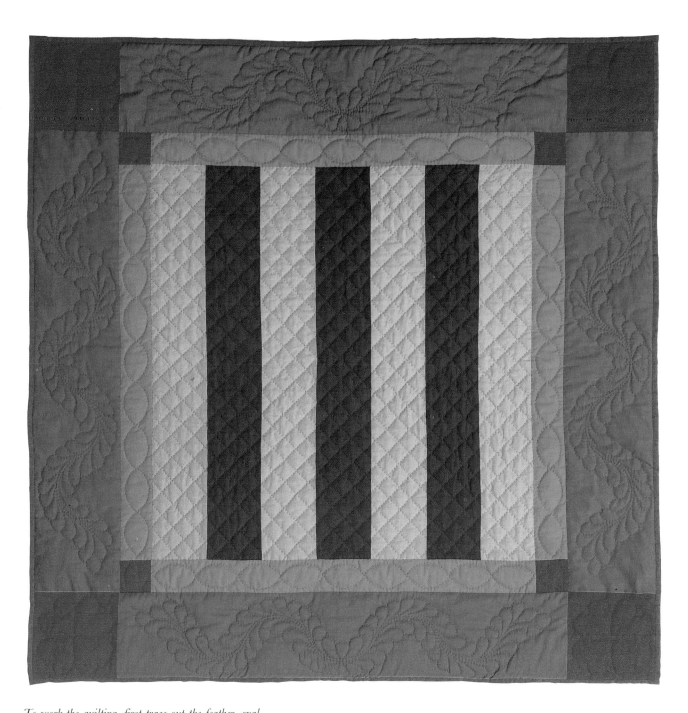

To work the quilting, first trace out the feather, oval
and heart designs. Reverse the feather and heart shapes
and continue the oval shapes to make a chain. Enlarge
all the designs using either the grid method described
on page 141 or a photocopier with an enlargement
facility. Mark the centre of each quilt border with a
trace tack (page 149) to help you line up the centre of
the quilting design accurately, making sure that you
leave an equal distance between the seam lines on each
side and allow sufficient space for the binding round
the edge of the finished quilt.

Crazy Patchwork Basket

Transform a plain wicker basket into a pretty yet practical showpiece with a crazy patchwork lining. Perfect to display fruit or vegetables in your kitchen or coloured soap and handtowels in your bathroom, the basket would also make the ideal gift for a friend with a new baby when filled with baby supplies.

Baskets are made around the world and come in a wonderful range of shapes and sizes. A rectangular basket like the one in the photograph is simple to line, but you could substitute a circular or oval one instead, or a smaller basket without the handle.

The lining is made from crazy patchwork. This technique is not only quick, easy and fun to do, but it provides a good way of using up small, irregularly shaped scraps of fabric left over from larger projects. Traditionally, crazy patchwork is embroidered with a variety of decorative stitches, but here, the patches are seamed together on the sewing machine for speed.

MATERIALS
- *Basket*
- *Calico to fit the outside measurement and depth of the basket, plus the base*
- *Selection of printed fabric scraps, pressed*
- *Length of 5cm (2in) bias binding slightly longer than the outside measurement of the basket*
- *Neutral sewing thread*
- *Narrow elastic*
- *2m (2yds) satin ribbon in two colours*

CUTTING OUT THE FABRIC
1 Measure the depth and width of the basket and add nearly double the depth so the lining will overlap the top generously. Measure the dimensions of base.
2 The basket lining is made in three pieces, one to cover the base and two identical pieces

which, together, cover the sides and overlap the top. The diagram shows how the pieces fit together. Cut out each piece from the calico, making each one slightly larger than your measurements to allow for seams.

MAKING THE PATCHWORK

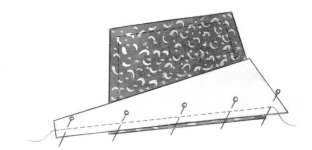

1 Place a scrap of printed fabric on the calico and pin in place. Select a second scrap and place this right sides together over the first patch. Pin the raw edges together, machine stitch, turn back and press.

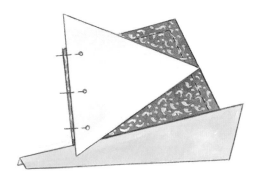

2 Continue pinning and stitching the patches together until the calico pieces are covered with printed scraps. You will find that it is not possible to make a seam along every raw edge of every patch, so in this case turn under the raw edge of the patch and machine stitch it to the calico working from the right side.

LINING THE BASKET
1 To shape the sides, place the two pieces of calico inside the basket with the patched sides towards the basket. Hold the fabric in place with masking tape and pin a series of darts to reduce the fullness in the sides until they fit the base. Machine stitch the darts, press and trim away any surplus fabric.

Simple yet eyecatching, this basket lined with crazy patchwork in bright, spring-like colours has a variety of uses. Perfect for holding fruit or vegetables in the kitchen or toiletries in the bathroom, the colour scheme of the patchwork is easily altered to suit your surroundings.

2 Place the side pieces back in the basket with the patched sides towards the basket. Place the base piece in the bottom of the basket, again with the patched side facing the basket. Pin the pieces together, remove from the basket and machine stitch together. Press the seams open. Don't forget to leave the centre seams to accommodate the handle.

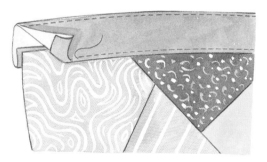

3 Bind (page 145) the edges of the centre seam along the portion which has been left

open. Then bind the remaining raw edge round the overlap with a 6mm (¼in) seam allowance. The extra fabric will form a channel for the elastic. Machine stitch close to the edge of the binding. Press the lining and place it in the basket. Thread narrow elastic through the binding channel, join the ends and stitch together securely.

4 To make the cover for the basket handle, stitch more patches together to make a long strip about 10cm (4in) wide and long enough to wrap round the handle and cover it completely. Trim and press under the raw edge along one side of the strip. Wind the strip round the handle, making sure that the raw edges along the remaining side of the strip are concealed under the pressed edge. Secure both ends with a few stitches and decorate the handle with ribbon bows, either two narrow or one wide.

Basque Belt

Wear this wonderfully creative belt low on the hips to give special flair to a simple dress. The belt uses a wide variety of materials and techniques including Suffolk puffs (page 146) as well as exploring the possibilities afforded by lace motifs, beads, sequins, ribbon and braid.

Worked in delicate pastel shades, the belt could be used to decorate a plain bridal gown or made in black and gold it would lend sophistication to a little black dress.

MATERIALS

- *Selection of scraps of plain and printed fabric including silk and lurex*
- *Lace motifs*
- *Scraps of ribbon and braid*
- *Assorted beads and sequins*
- *25cm (10in) medium weight non-woven interfacing 90cm (36in)-wide*
- *25cm (10in) lining fabric 90cm (36in) wide*
- *Hooks and eyes or touch-and-close fastening*

MAKING THE BELT

1 Trace off the belt template on page 78 and enlarge it to fit round your hips using the method shown on page 141. Cut the shape out of the interfacing, adding a seam allowance of 12mm ($\frac{1}{2}$in) all round.
2 Working from one end of the belt, cover the interfacing with crazy patchwork (page 39).

MAKING AND ADDING THE DECORATION

1 Make Suffolk puffs (page 146) from either silk or lurex fabric, cutting the circles 10cm (4in) in diameter.

This unusual belt was designed and made by Trudi Billingsley, an Australian quilter, in colours inspired by the underwater life of the Great Barrier Reef. Here, flower and leaf shapes are applied to a crazy patchwork base, but you could substitute fish, coral and seaweed shapes to echo the nautical theme.

2 To make the flower and leaf motifs, trace off the templates and cut them from the leftover interfacing, cutting out just outside the tracing line. Pin a piece of fabric to the back of each shape, turn over and machine in straight stitch around the tracing line and add veins or any other details. Turn over so the right side of the shape is facing you, machine zigzag over the lines of straight stitching. Trim surplus fabric and interfacing away round the shape close to the stitching.

3 Colour the lace motifs with paint and allow them to dry.

4 Place the decorative components on the belt and move them around until you are happy with the arrangement. Secure them with hand

or machine stitching and decorate with groups of beads and sequins. Attach the hanging leaf shapes after the belt has been lined.

FINISHING THE BELT

1 Cut out the lining, remembering to add the seam allowance. Place the lining over the right side of the belt, pin, tack and machine stitch together leaving one end open.

2 Trim the seam allowance and clip the curves (page 151). Turn the belt to the right side through the opening and slip stitch (page 148) the opening closed. Add any hanging leaves at this stage. Finally, try on the belt and add hooks and eyes or a touch-and-close fastener at each end.

Before you begin cutting and stitching, measure around your hips where you will be wearing the belt and enlarge the pattern to this size. After attaching the lining, trim down the seam allowance and the corners and clip into the curves. This will reduce the bulk of the surplus fabric and allow the fabric layers to curve smoothly.

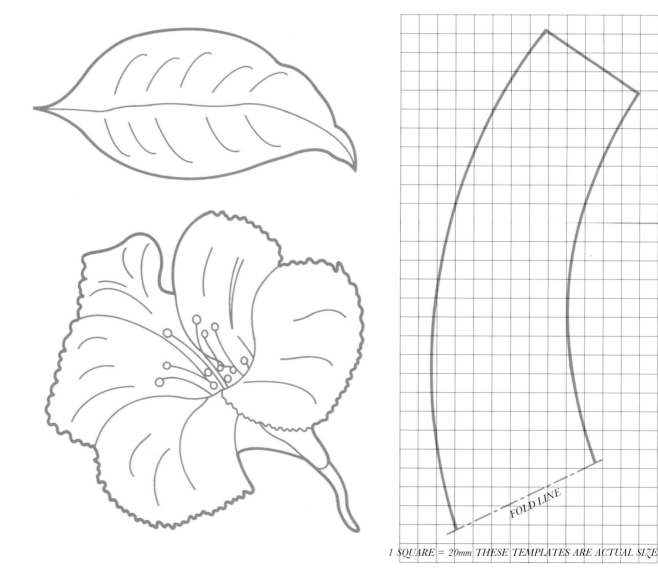

1 SQUARE = 20mm THESE TEMPLATES ARE ACTUAL SIZE

Celtic
Evening
Bag

*When buying fabric to
make this design, choose
a fine cotton lawn so the
bias strip curves without
puckering and is perfectly
flat when finally stitched
in position.*

Make this evening bag from silk fabric. The design is a variation of a Celtic True Lover's Knot and it would work equally well as a quilting design or for Italian quilting (page 46). Celtic designs are characterized by repeating lines which weave over and under each other and here the design is carried out using bias strips.

MATERIALS

- *30cm (12in) blue dupion silk 115cm (45in) wide*
- *30cm (12in) lining fabric 115cm (45in) wide*
- *50cm (20in) black cotton lawn 115cm (45in) wide*
- *30cm (12in) pelmet weight (heavy-weight) non-woven interfacing*
- *1m (39in) No 2 (2mm) cotton piping cord*
- *1m (39in) black cord for shoulder strap*
- *6mm (¼in) Celtic bar (bias press bar) (page 145)*
- *Black sewing thread*
- *Button*
- *Hand – or ready-made tassel (page 146)*
- *Liquid fray-check*
- *Black felt-tipped pen with a fine point*
- *White or gold pencil*
- *Fabric glue*
- *2 black beads (optional)*

TRANSFERRING THE DESIGN

1 Trace off the Celtic design with the black felt pen and enlarge to 23 cm (9 in) diameter. Cut out two pieces of silk 28cm (11in) square. Squeeze a thin line of liquid fray-check on to the raw edges.

2 Transfer the design on to one piece of silk by taping the tracing and the fabric on to the window or a light box. Trace the design with a white or gold pencil.

MAKING THE BLACK STRIP

1 Cut the black fabric into bias strips (page 144) 2cm (⅞in) wide until you have sufficient pieces to measure 3.5m (3¾yd).

2 Fold the strips in half lengthways and make a 3mm (⅛in) seam along the edge. Slip the Celtic bar (bias press bar) inside the tube, fold the seam allowance over to one side and press. Slide the bar along the tubes until all have been pressed, turn them over and press the other side. Leave a 1m (39in) length to one side for the piping.

WORKING THE DESIGN

1 Mark the 'under' junctions on the transferred design with stationer's dots.
As you stitch the black strip down along the design lines, stop at every 'under' junction and pass the needle along without making any stitches. This will allow you to weave the strip under at the junction and keep the sequence correct.

2 Begin at the position marked by the arrow on the diagram. Pin a short section of the black strip in position on the design and slip stitch (page 148) it to the background with black sewing thread, sewing the inner curve first, then the outer curve which will stretch.

3 When you reach a corner of the design, fold the bias as with a mitred corner (page 144) and hold the point in place with a stitch. Continue stitching the black strip to the background until the design is finished, ending at an 'under' junction. Cut the strip and tuck the end neatly out of sight, securing it with a few stitches. Press from the wrong side.

MAKING UP THE BAG

1 Cut two circles from the interfacing to fit inside the outer line on the diagram. Draw the stitching line (this is the inner circle on the diagram) on the interfacing in pencil. Cut out 'v' shapes from round the outer edge, taking care not to cut into the stitching line. Tack the back and front on to the interfacings, following the stitching line. Trim the silk to fit the interfacing circles.

2 Make piping from the remaining black lawn strip and the piping cord as shown on page 145. Make a loop for the button from black cord or by making a rouleau (page 145) and secure it at the centre of the opening on the back with a few stitches.

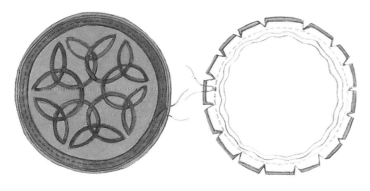

tack in position. Machine stitch the piping, turn back the seam allowances and hold in place with fabric glue. Put the back and front on a flat surface and cover with some heavy books until the glue has dried.

4 Cut out the lining and stitch together, leaving a gap for the opening. Cut 'v' shapes out of the seam allowance. Place the bag back and front together wrong side to wrong side, matching up the opening. Slip stitch (page 148) together from the back. Sew the cord on either side of the opening.

5 Slip the lining inside the bag and slip stitch along the opening. Sew on button. Decorate with a tassel and beads either side of opening.

3 Cut 20cm (8in) from the piping to fit around the opening of the back of the bag and tack in position. Measure a circle of piping to fit around the front of the bag and

1 SQUARE = 8mm (½in)

Seminole Patchwork Braces

Seminole patchwork takes its name from the Seminole Indians of Florida who worked the intricate looking technique on their clothing. In fact, the technique is much simpler than it appears. Today, the Seminole Indians stitch their patchwork designs mainly for the tourist market, but patchworkers throughout the world are making and adapting their brilliantly colourful designs using this technique.

The technique works best with solid coloured fabric, particularly when contrasted with black set between stripes of plain colours. Depending on the tones of the fabric, striking three-dimensional effects can appear. The two designs used on the braces are achieved by machine stitching various widths of fabric strips together, then cutting these strips at right angles or at 45 degrees and finally rejoining the pieces. As with other forms of strip patchwork, accurate measuring and cutting is essential, but the use of a rotary cutter and self-healing cutting mat will speed up this process considerably.

MATERIALS
- *20cm (8in) each of green, blue and red cotton fabric 115cm (45in) wide*
- *Red felt for lining*
- *Three 2.5cm (1in) braces clips*
- *Neutral and red cotton sewing thread*
- *Rotary cutter*
- *Self-healing cutting mat*

The intricate nature of Seminole patchwork uses many pieces of fabric so the resulting patchwork is rather heavy and is best used in small pieces. Here, the technique is used to make an unusual pair of braces. Made to the measurements given here, the braces will fit a medium size person, but can easily be lengthened by adding more patches to the single back strap.

CUTTING AND JOINING THE STRIPS

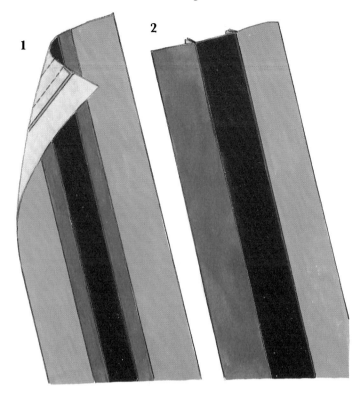

square. Measure along the two long edges of the strips and divide the strips into 32mm (1¼in) sections. Cut into sections.

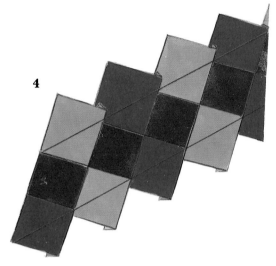

4 Following the diagram, join the sections together using the chain piecing method described on page 143 until each strip measures 71cm (28in).

1 Cutting right across the width of the fabric, cut 2 blue strips 4cm (1½in) wide; 2 blue strips 2cm (¾in) wide; 4 green strips 4cm (1½in) wide; 3 red strips 32mm (1¼in) wide.
2 Using a neutral thread, join the strips together with a seam allowance of 6mm (¼in), following the diagrams. Press the seam allowances to one side.

MAKING THE CENTRE BACK BRACE

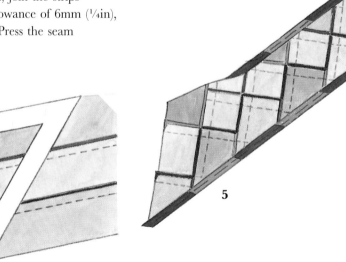

MAKING THE TWO FRONT BRACES

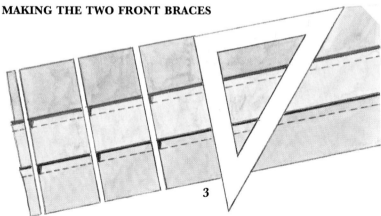

3 Place the strips on a flat surface and straighten one end of each strip with a set

5 Follow steps 1 and 3 (above) but this time divide the strip into 45mm (1¾in) sections and join together following diagram 6 until the strip is 30cm (12in) long.

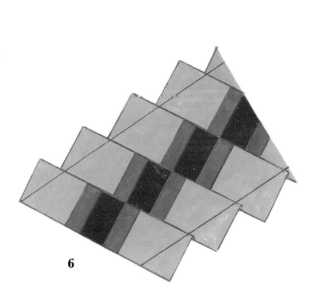

6

6 Press all the seams in one direction, then turn under and press a seam allowance of 6mm (¼in) all round. Run a tacking (basting) stitch along each folded under edge, making sure the edges remain straight, so the felt backing (lining) will conceal the rough edges.

7

7 Stitch the two front braces together along the seamline indicated. Press the seam open. Position the seam at the centre top of the back brace. Pin, tack and stitch in position.

Finishing the braces

8 Thread a clip on to the end of each strip, turn over the seam allowance and slip stitch (page 148) in place. Line the back of the braces with pieces of felt cut slightly smaller and slip stitched in position.

8

R e d
C e n t r e

Simply constructed from three hinged wooden frames, this patchwork screen is an unusual project suitable for the ambitious quilter. The design represents Australia's Ayers Rock which lies at the centre of this huge country. The rock is so large that it can be seen from miles away, towering over the flat bushland. Although the heat is intense during the day, temperatures drop suddenly and it is very cold at night. The surface of the rock is pitted by deep gulleys which have been worn down its sides by condensation. The real magic occurs as the sun rises and sets, casting glowing reflections, dramatic shadows and areas of brilliant colour on to the rock's surface.

The screen uses a mixture of fabric, including some Aboriginal designs, but you could substitute any brightly coloured printed fabric. If you prefer to make the design up as a quilted wallhanging rather than as a screen, trace off and enlarge the designs on page 141 without leaving a gap between the panels.

MATERIALS FOR THE PANELS

- *30cm (12in) cotton fabric 115cm (45in) wide in each of 8 plain colours and 8 prints*
- *1m (39in) black cotton fabric 115cm (45in) wide*
- *30cm (12in) red spotted cotton fabric 115cm (45in) wide*
- *10cm (4in) plain red cotton fabric 115cm (45in) wide*
- *1.7m (2yds) backing fabric 115cm (45in) wide*
- *1.7m (2yds) needlepunch (loomtex) wadding 115cm (45mm) wide*
- *10cm (4in) fusible bonding web*
- *Small red beads (optional)*
- *Neutral sewing thread*
- *Transparent nylon thread and neutral polyester thread for machine quilting*
- *12mm (½in) wide masking tape*
- *Dressmakers' pattern paper joined to make a piece 125cm × 132cm (49in × 52in)*
- *Sharp HB pencil*

MAKING THE TEMPLATES

1 Trace off the design on page 88 and enlarge it to the correct dimensions using the grid method shown on page 141. Keep the tracing as this will act as your key.

2 Number each shape and add the balance marks (page 151) around the circle, grain lines and other markings. Transfer all the information and cut into templates.

MAKING THE PANELS

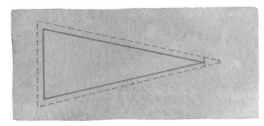

1 Select your fabric and attach a small sample of each piece to your traced design. Place the templates on the wrong side of the fabric and draw round them with a sharp HB pencil, making sure the grain lines are correct. Put in balance marks and also mark exactly where to stop stitching on shapes with a tapering point. Check that the shapes are in the correct fabric.

2 Cut out the pieces adding a 6mm (¼in) seam allowance. Clip (page 151) into the seam allowance round the edge of the circle. Divide them into three piles, one for each panel.

3 To make the gulley shape across the circle, bond the red fabric shape to the circle using fusible bonding web very securely to ensure it is are stuck firmly and will not come off. Secure the gulley by machine satin stitching along the edges.

4 Join each panel separately. Lay out the pieces in the correct order, then pin, tack and machine stitch them together. Press each seam

This screen uses a combination of brightly patterned and coloured fabrics, including some modern Aboriginal designs. Choose your selection of fabrics carefully, investigating the huge variety of dress-weight cottons which are now available in the shops. If you would rather make up the design as a wallhanging, simply continue the design right across the gaps left to accommodate the wooden frame.

open after stitching and trim away surplus fabric where several points meet. Where there are several joins round the circle, stitch to a join and, leaving the needle in the fabric, lift the presser foot and push any surplus fabric out of the way. Drop the presser foot and continue stitching. In this case, press the seam allowances towards the circle.

QUILTING THE PANELS

1 Press all the panels well on both sides of the fabric. Check that the design matches at the sides and make any adjustments at this stage.

Cut out the wadding and backing fabric slightly larger than the panels.

2 Assemble and tack the layers together (page 48). Machine quilt (page 143) the panels using nylon thread on the top and polyester thread in the bobbin. Mark out the quilting lines with strips of masking tape and sew along the edge. (Don't leave the masking tape in position overnight or for a long period of time as the glue can mark the fabric.) Sew beads on to the spotted red centre, if required. Attach the binding, folding it to the back so that it does not show on the front.

When setting in the black areas of this design, take care to snip into the corners to be stretched and cut a small 'V' shape from the corners to be reduced. Stitch the seams, working from the centre of the design outwards, then press them open and carefully trim away surplus fabric at the places where several points meet.

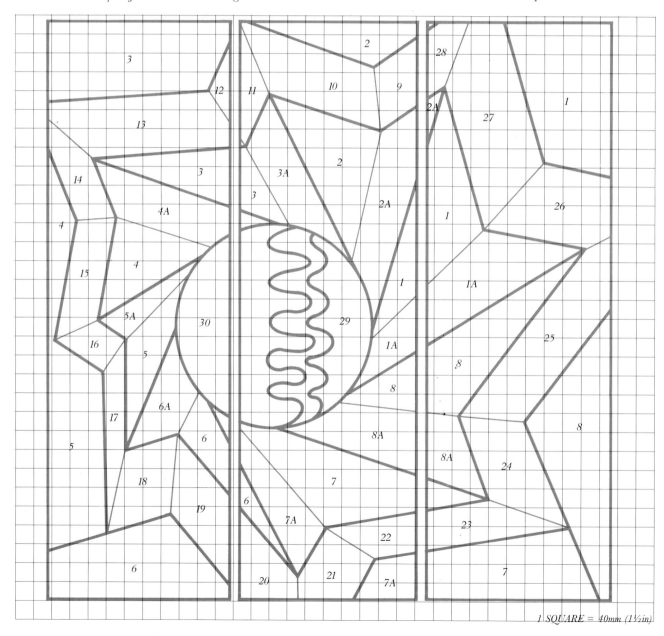

1 SQUARE = 40mm (1½in)

Each of the panels below measures 39cm × 120cm (15½in × 48in) with a gap of 45mm (1½in) below.

ASSEMBLING THE SCREEN

1 Pin the sleeves (page 150) to the top and bottom of each panel, incorporating them into the binding. Each sleeve is passed over a dowel rod and secured after the screen is painted. Fold the binding over the rod so it cannot be seen from the front and slip stitch (page 148) in place.

2 Measure the panels, then make the screen up as shown below. Pin the panels in position folding the sleeve edges over the dowel rods and on to the back of the panels. Slip stitch them in place.

THE SCREEN

This very simple screen consists of three hinged frames made from one size of planed stripwood and one diameter of dowel rod, both obtainable from DIY stores and timber merchants.

Soft woods, such as pine, are the least expensive and these work well if you are going to paint the screen. Ramin and beech cost more than pine, but retain their natural colour when varnished and have more regular grain markings. The sizes marked on dowel rod in the shop are not always accurate, so check that you have a drill to match the size.

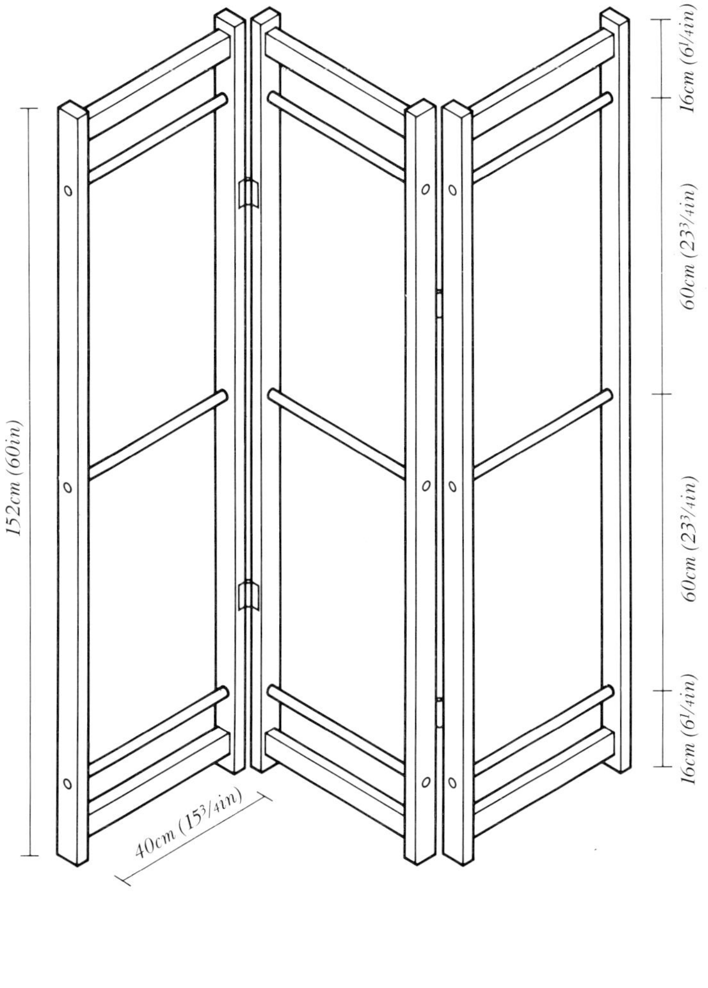

MATERIALS

● *Planed stripwood 18mm × 45mm (¾in × 1¾in)*
● *Dowel rod 16mm (⅝in) in diameter*
● *45mm (2in) brass hinges*
● *38mm (1½in) no 8 wood screws*
● *18mm (¾in) panel pins*
● *Wood glue*
● *Plastic filler*

CUTTING THE WOOD

Cut 6 uprights 152cm (60in) in length from the stripwood and 6 cross bars 40cm (15¾in) in length. Cut 6 pieces of dowel rod 46cm (18in) in length.

ASSEMBLING THE SCREEN

1 Clamp the uprights together in pairs and drill holes through both pieces matching the diameter of the dowel rod. The holes should be 16cm (6¼in) from the top and 16cm (6¼in) from the bottom of each upright. Sandpaper all the pieces for a smooth finish.

2 Assemble each frame as shown in the diagram (left), glueing and screwing the crossbars into place and allowing the dowels to project beyond the frame uprights. Drive panel pins through the rear edge of each upright to fix the dowels in place. If you have a large bench or kitchen table, clamp the frame in position to help accurate assembly. Check for squareness by measuring the two corner-to-corner diagonals, and also check that the cross bar lengths match the finished width of your panels.

3 When the glue is dry, saw off the projecting dowels flush with the uprights and fill all holes and flaws with plastic filler. When this has hardened, finish off with sandpaper.

4 Position and screw on the hinges. Remember the screen zigzags, so the hinges must be on opposite sides of the uprights. Paint, varnish or stain the wood.

Colourful Story

This colourful quilted wallhanging was designed by Sheila Yale, British Designer Quilter, and it is based on well-known sayings which use colour to describe feelings – 'In a brown study, feeling blue and green with envy, she saw red, swore black was white and ended up tickled pink'.

The quilt incorporates a traditional block (Shoofly) which is adapted and placed within the overall design, then infilled with strips, squares and triangles of fabric. Three-dimensional prairie points, quilting and the addition of buttons add textural interest to the surface and contrast well with the brightly coloured printed fabric. Sheila chose her selection of fabric by concentrating on good and unusual colour combinations, changes of scale and tone, together with a variety of printed designs. She works in units, pinning her work to a white-painted, softboard wall. This allows her to stand back and judge how the design is progressing as a whole, adding and removing sections as necessary.

The wall hanging should only be attempted by an experienced quilter. Although the instructions for drawing up the design are given in some detail, fabric quantities are not stated as the design is intended as a starting point which you can expand to incorporate your own creative selection of fabric.

The finished wallhanging measures 140cm × 119cm (55in × 47in).

MATERIALS

- *Good selection of printed cotton fabric*
- *125cm (50in) cotton backing fabric 150cm (60in) wide*
- *150cm (60in) thick polyester wadding 150cm (60in) wide*
- *8 pink buttons*
- *Neutral sewing thread*
- *Matching and contrasting quilting threads*
- *Squared paper*
- *Dressmakers' pattern paper*

DRAWING UP YOUR DESIGN

1 Trace off the plan shown on page 93. Decide what size you would like the wallhanging to be and rule up squared paper to scale. Choose a traditional block, adapt it and pencil in at the positions shown on the plan.

2 Continue the design by extending lines from the blocks to the edges of the hanging, sub-dividing the areas to give a balanced design. The plain areas shown on the plan can be filled with all sorts of sub-divisions, so be as inventive as you like within these spaces.

3 When you are happy with the arrangement of shapes, transfer your design to dressmaker's pattern paper to make a full-size design. At this stage, you may like to make adjustments both to balance the design and also to simplify the piecing process.

MAKING THE TEMPLATES

This design can be worked using paper templates traced off from your full-size design, or you might find it helpful to cut some of the shapes from template plastic so that you can isolate interesting areas on the printed fabric.

MAKING UP THE TOP

1 Lay out all the fabrics you have chosen in a rough approximation of the finished design. You may like to attach a small piece of fabric to each of the shapes on the full-size design, or you may prefer to work in a more random fashion.

2 Begin by machine stitching the traditional blocks together in the usual way, pressing the seams open. Pin the blocks on to your full-size plan. Continue cutting shapes out of the fabric and pinning them on to the design in the same way. Squares of fabric which have been folded over twice diagonally can be incorporated into the seams, as in the pink area on the photograph, together with strips of prairie points (page 146).

3 When you are happy with one section of the hanging, pin and machine stitch the pieces together, pressing each seam after it has been stitched. Work section by section until the top is complete. Press well on both sides.

In this delightful quilt, Sheila Yale takes well-known sayings which mention colour as the starting point for her design. Sheila works exclusively in patterned fabrics and has a huge collection of fabric pieces stored in colour-related groups in polythene bags. The bags are arranged in rows in a cupboard, exactly like a library of books. Sheila's workroom also contains inspirational scrap books bursting with ideas and many designs already worked out on paper.

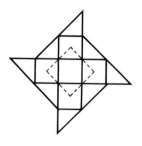

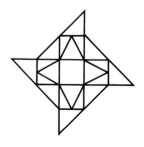

QUILTING THE TOP

1 Cut the backing fabric and the wadding slightly larger than the top. Tack the layers together (page 143).

2 The wallhanging can be quilted on a frame (page 140) or in the hand (page 147). For the design, use a combination of straight lines to echo some of the shapes formed by the patches plus lines which follow some of the more dominant designs printed on the fabric. Use a variety of coloured threads and add buttons to make the surface of the hanging more interesting.

FINISHING THE HANGING

1 Cut four binding strips 35mm (1½in) wide and slightly longer than each side of the top. Attach these as described on page 145.

2 To hang the wallhanging, make a fabric sleeve and attach it to the back as shown and described on page 150.

Two adaptations of the traditional block 'Shoofly' as shown on page 90 are incorporated into this quilt design. Many of the hundreds of traditional block patterns can be used in this way, creating several variations lengthening or shortening existing lines and adding or removing others.

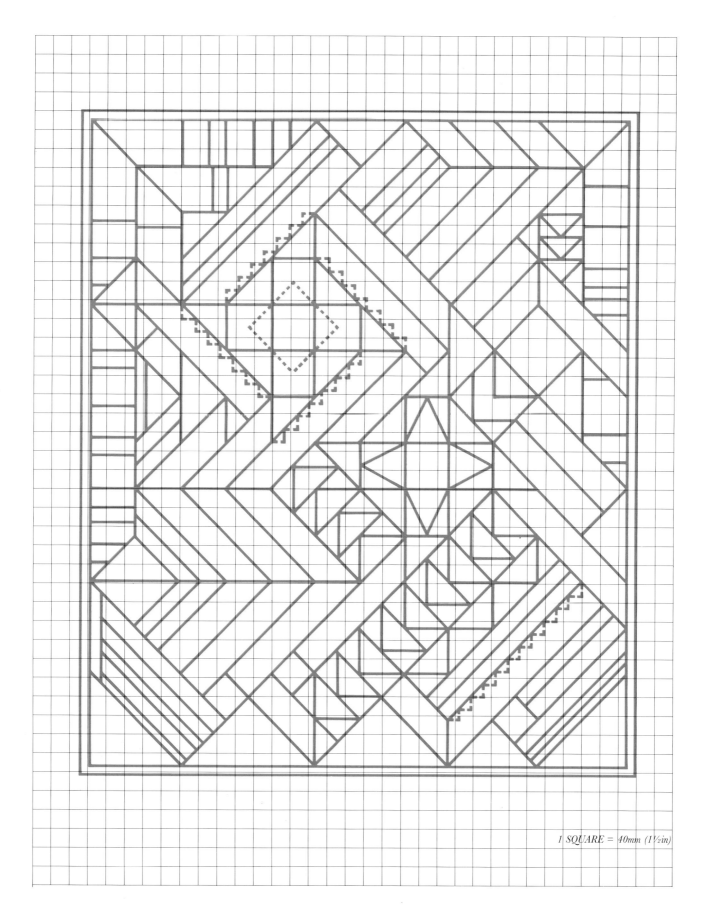

1 SQUARE = 40mm (1½in)

Curved Patchwork Cushion

This pure silk cushion cover features a boldly curving design which can be simplified to suit the less experienced stitcher by joining together templates one, two and three to make a larger, easy to handle piece.

The cushion cover measures just under 40cm (16in), but there are two simple ways to make it larger. Either enlarge the design to the required size when you are drawing it up from the diagram on page 96, or join extra strips of fabric to each side using the log cabin technique described on page 40. When changing the original dimensions, remember that you will need more fabric. Curved shapes take slightly more fabric than straight-sided patchwork shapes as they need to be cut across the bias of the fabric. For this design, you could use up any scraps of left-over silk to make the smaller shapes, adding new fabric for the large shapes and the backing.

For an alternative effect, you could make up this cushion in a single colour using several types of fabric to give textural interest. It's unwise to vary the weight of the fabric too much, but a mixture of satin, woven cotton, taffeta, glazed cotton and cotton twill would look stunning, with the surface textures catching and reflecting the light at different angles.

To achieve a crisp, distortion-free result, always make sure that the straight grain of the fabric runs in the correct direction as shown in the diagram on page 96. Marking balance marks (page 96) in the seam allowance and clipping the seam allowance along the curves (page 151) will ensure that the pieces fit together perfectly.

This cushion is made from pure silk in a selection of rich colours. As the design is suitable for a first attempt at curved patchwork, beginners could substitute less expensive cotton for the silk and also join together templates one, two and three before cutting out to make a large piece which will be easier to handle.

MATERIALS
- *Scraps of silk fabric with two pieces at least 32cm (12½in) square.*
- *50cm (20in) silk or cotton backing fabric 115cm (45in) wide*
- *50cm (20in) square of wadding*
- *50cm (20in) square of muslin*
- *36cm (14in) zip fastener to match backing fabric*
- *Silk sewing thread to match the predominant fabric colour*
- *Liquid fray-check*
- *Cushion pad*
- *Dressmaker's pattern paper*
- *Sharp HB pencil*
- *Felt-tip pen with a fine point*
- *Sandpaper board*

CUTTING THE TEMPLATES AND FABRIC

1 Trace off the template design on page 96 and enlarge it (page 141) to the required size. (The design is shown reversed on page 96 so it is ready to trace off and will appear the correct way round.)

2 Draw in the balance marks. Number each piece and draw in the grain lines. Cut up your design to make a set of paper templates.

3 Place a piece of fabric on the sandpaper board with the wrong side facing and position the appropriate template on top, checking the grain lines. Pin the paper to the fabric and draw round the edge using a sharp HB pencil. Draw in a 6mm (¼in) seam allowance round the edge plus the balance marks. Repeat for each template.

4 Before cutting out the silk, squeeze a fine line of liquid fray-check along the cutting lines which fall on the straight grain of the fabric. The bias cuts will not fray.

5 Wait until the liquid is completely dry, then cut out.

PATCHING THE CUSHION FRONT

1 Join the pieces by matching and pinning the balance marks together first, then add extra pins evenly along the seam. Tack along the stitching line and leave the pins in position at each end of the seam to help keep the edges of the front straight. Clip the curves.

2 Join the pieces in the following order: a 1, 2 and 3; b 5, 6 and 7; c 10 and 11; d 8, 9 and 10/11. Press the seam allowances of the joined pieces into the curves. Add 5/6/7 to piece 4 and then add 8/9/10/11 to the same piece. Press as above. Finally add 1/2/3 to complete the cushion front.

QUILTING THE CUSHION FRONT

1 Press the front well, clipping any curved seams as necessary to make them lie flat.

Sandwich the wadding between the front and the muslin and tack the layers together following the diagram on page 143.

2 Quilt (page 147) the front following the curved lines, working the lines of quilting stitches about 3mm ($\frac{1}{8}$in) away from the seams. Do not press the quilting.

3 To make up the cushion cover, follow the illustrated instructions on page 145. You can, of course, always use cotton, as it is a more practical alternative to silk.

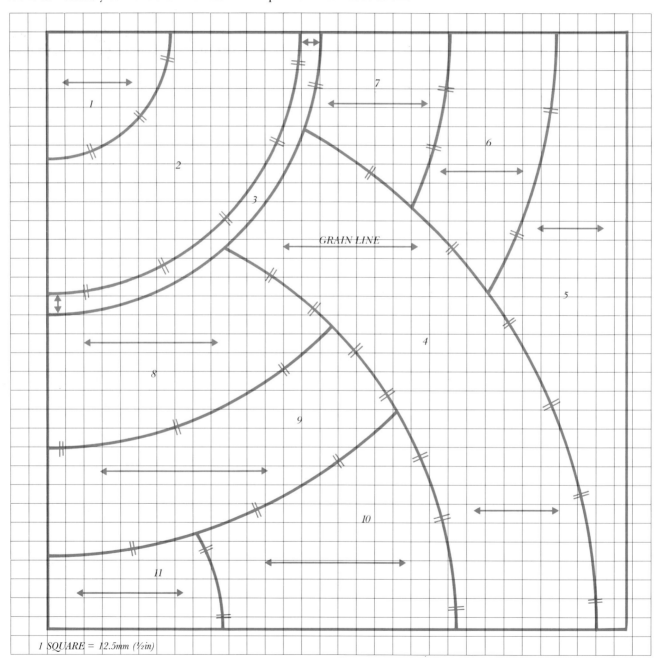

1 SQUARE = 12.5mm ($\frac{1}{2}$in)

Islamic
Mat

Made over papers, this Islamic inspired design is a step onwards from the hexagon flower shapes used in the traditional 'Grandmothers Garden' designs.

Although the hexagon is the most popular form, many other geometric shapes such as triangles and diamonds can be used as well. This way of joining patchwork is known as the English method and it consists of fabric patches which are tacked over paper shapes, then hand-stitched together. The main reason for using this technique is to join angles which would be difficult to work on the machine.

Old letters were traditionally used to make the paper shapes and good quality modern writing paper is about the right thickness for this purpose.

If you decide to do this too, be sure to place the written side of the paper away from the fabric so that the ink does not stain the front of your work.

A good way to practise this technique is to cut out and tack seven hexagon patches. Assemble six patches in a circle round the seventh and stitch them together to make a simple flower shape.

Two flowers joined and stuffed make an attractive pincushion which can be decorated with pearl beads at each corner and then, if you wish, finished off with one or more initials spelled out in glass-headed pins in the centre. The finished mat shown here measures just over 40cm (16in) across.

The mat is made in 7 colours of shot silk to enhance the play of light across the surface. As the fabric grain catches the light, different shades emerge from the fabric. When using pure silk fabric, always choose pure silk sewing thread.

MATERIALS

- *25cm (10in) of shot silk fabric 90cm (36in) wide in 7 colours*
- *Firm non-woven interfacing*
- *50cm (20in) square of backing fabric, preferably silk*
- *Tacking thread*
- *Silk sewing threads to match the predominant fabric colours*
- *Template plastic*
- *Waterproof marker with a fine point*
- *Stiff paper*
- *Sharp HB pencil*
- *Liquid fray-check*
- *30cm (12in) polystyrene tile*
- *Sandpaper board*

CUTTING THE TEMPLATES AND PATCHWORK PAPERS

1 Enlarge the template shapes on to template plastic. Mark the grain line on each shape and number the shapes using a waterproof marker. Carefully cut out each template with a pair of paper scissors.

2 To make the patchwork papers, place the plastic templates on the stiff paper and draw round the edge with a sharp HB pencil. Cut out the papers using paper scissors or a craft knife and straight edge. You will need to cut the following quantities of each shape: 8 each of shapes 1, 2, 5, 6 and 8; 16 each of shapes 3 and 4; 64 of shape 7.

MAKING THE PATCHES

1 Place a piece of fabric with wrong side facing upwards on the sandpaper board. Draw round the plastic template the correct number of times for the first shape, allowing a seam allowance of 6mm (¼in) round each one and making sure the grain runs the same way across each shape. Repeat for each shape.

2 Before cutting out the silk, squeeze a fine line of liquid fray-check along the cutting lines which fall on the straight grain. The bias cuts will not fray. Wait until the liquid is completely dry, then cut out the shapes using sharp scissors.

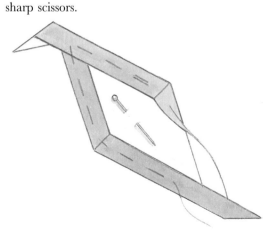

3 Place a patchwork paper on the wrong side of a fabric shape and pin. Fold the seam allowance of the fabric over the paper and tack round the shape, paying special attention to folding in the corners neatly. Repeat until you have the required number of patches.

JOINING THE PATCHES

1 Pin the patches on to the polystyrene tile in the correct sequence shown in the plan below. Start sewing the patches together working outwards from the centre of the eight-pointed star and finishing with the bands.

2 Place the first two patches together, right sides facing. Make a small knot at the end of your thread and slide the needle under the seam allowance so it emerges at the corner of the patch.

3 Matching the edges, sew the patches together with small oversewing stitches (page 148). The stitches should be so small that you see only a tiny stitch on the right side when the patches are opened out.

4 Continue joining the patches in sequence until the design is complete.

MAKING UP THE MAT

1 Press the patchwork, carefully remove the tacking stitches and the papers, then press again. Cut out a piece of interfacing slightly smaller than the patchwork and tack it to the wrong side of the top. Cut out a piece of backing fabric slightly larger than the patchwork and mark the shape of the mat on the wrong side of the fabric with the HB pencil.

2 Press the seam allowance to the wrong side along the pencil lines. Pin the back and front together with the wrong sides facing and carefully ladder stitch (page 148) together.

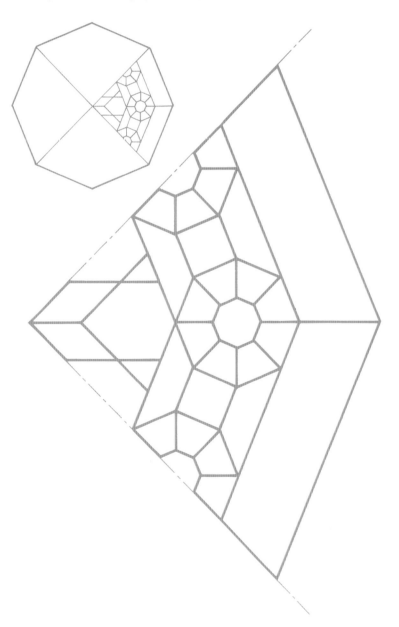

H u g e   C u r v e s

Designed with the help of a computer (page 63), the design on this single bed quilt creates a three-dimensional pattern which is accentuated by the use of light and dark tones of two colours. Two simple curves were drawn on paper and then scanned into the computer. Several hundred variations were created as the computer flipped, rotated and transposed the curves.

There are 40 blocks in the single size quilt shown here, but the size can be made larger or smaller to fit a different size of bed by adding or subtracting more blocks at each side.

The finished quilt measures 246cm × 153cm (92in × 60in) and is really only suitable for an experienced quilter.

MATERIALS
- *2.50m (2½yd) pink cotton fabric 115cm (45in) wide*
- *90cm (1yd) printed cotton fabric 115cm (45in) wide in two shades of light blue and two shades of light green*
- *40cm (16in) printed cotton fabric 115cm (45in) wide in two shades of darker blue and two shades of darker green*
- *244cm × 163cm (100in × 64in) backing fabric, joined as necessary*
- *244cm × 163cm (100in × 64in) wadding, joined as necessary*
- *Sewing thread in a neutral colour*
- *Quilting threads to blend with the pink, blue and green fabric*
- *Template plastic*
- *Waterproof marker with a fine point*
- *Sharp HB pencil*
- *Red and blue self-adhesive spots*

MAKING THE TEMPLATES
1 Trace off the block on page 103 and enlarge it to 30cm (12in) using the grid method on page 141. Tape the enlargement to a window and trace a reverse block.

2 Using the waterproof marker, trace the two blocks on to template plastic, number them and add the balance marks (page 151). You will find it much easier to keep track of the blocks if you mark one set with red self-adhesive spots and the other set with blue spots. Number the red spots 1–9 and the blue spots 11–19.

CUTTING OUT THE FABRIC
1 Make a block plan to show the four variations on the basic block. Refer to the quilt plan on page 103 and decide which fabric to use for each block. Stick a small piece of the correct fabric on to each area on the block plan.

2 Cut binding strips 32mm (1¼in) wide from the pink fabric. Cut two 245cm (96½in) long and two 153cm (60½in) long. These strips can be joined to make the correct lengths.

3 On the wrong side of the fabric, draw round each template using a sharp HB pencil taking care to keep the fabric grain straight. Leave room between each piece for a 6mm (¼in) seam allowance all round. Transfer all the balance marks to the seam allowance and before cutting out, stick the appropriate red or blue spot on to the shape and number the spot. Cut out enough patches to make up 40 blocks.

PIECING THE QUILT TOP
1 Put the numbered patches into separate piles. Before you begin to sew, you will need to snip into the tight curve indicated by an arrow on the template. This will allow the fabric to stretch as you sew.

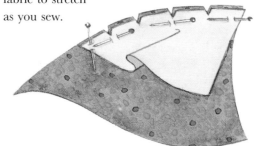

2 Using the chain piecing method described on page 143 and matching the balance marks, join together shapes 14 and 13; 12 and 15; 4

The three-dimensional effect of ribbon shapes curving and interweaving over this quilt was created with the help of a computer. Carefully chosen colours and curved quilting lines enhance the feeling of depth and movement of the patterned shapes, while the plain pink background is held back by straight quilted lines. To make this design fit a larger bed, add extra blocks and wide border strips.

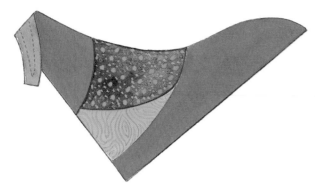

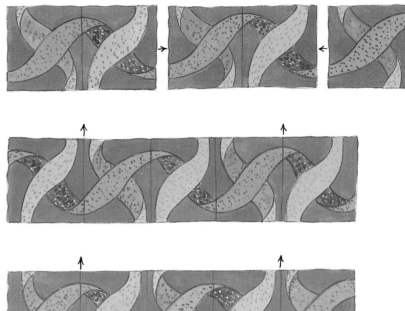

and 3; 2 and 5. Press before joining 17 and 18 to 14/13; 19 and 16 to 12/15; 7 and 8 to 4/3; 9 and 6 to 2/5. Press and finally join these pieces to both sides of 1 and 11, matching the balance marks (page 151).

3 Each block should now measure 30cm (12in) plus the seam allowance. If any of the blocks are incorrect, unpick suspect seams and re-stitch. Press seams carefully, taking care not to stretch the fabric along the curves.

4 Following the quilt plan opposite, join the blocks together in strips, then join the strips together. Pin the blocks together vertically through the seam allowances at the junctions where the curved shapes flow into the adjacent blocks so that the seams will match correctly. Machine stitch, check each seam then press it open. When all the blocks are joined together, give the quilt top a final press on both sides of the fabric.

QUILTING THE TOP

1 The quilting design should enhance the curved piecing, but a simple solution would be to quilt on either side of the seam lines and once or twice through the centres of the shapes. Mark up your quilting design following the instructions on page 141. A quilting design is given in the block shown on the opposite page.

2 Guide lines for assembling and tacking the layers of fabric and wadding together are given on page 143 with advice on quilting on page 147. When all the quilting has been completed, add the binding to finish off the quilt (page 143) and don't forget to sign your quilt with a label (page 8) attached to the back of the quilt.

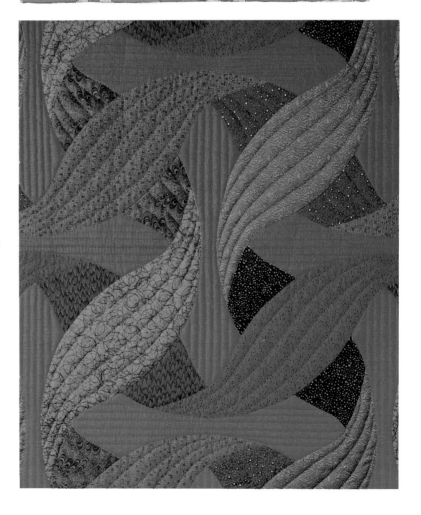

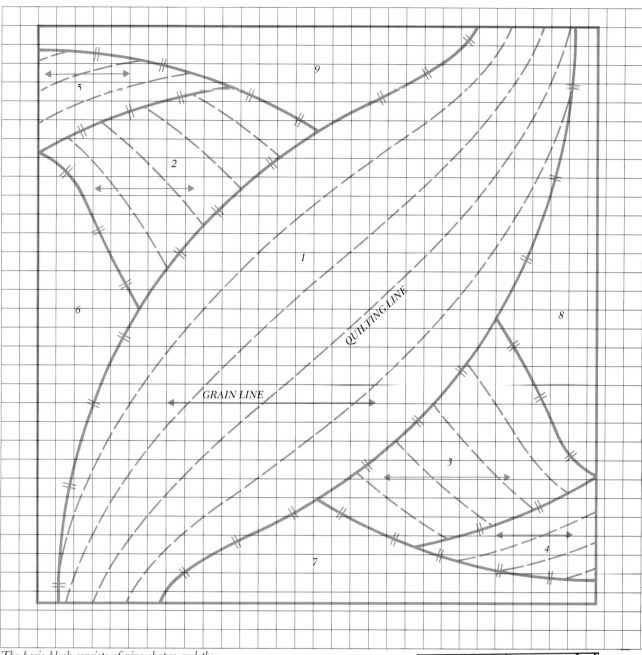

The basic block consists of nine shapes and the intricate design is made by reversing and rotating this block. Make two sets of templates, numbering one set from one to nine and the second, reverse set from eleven to nineteen, using two colours of stationer's dots to avoid confusion. Make sure you add balance marks and numbers to the block before cutting it up.

The block shown above corresponds to the green curled ribbon shapes (top right and bottom left) in the photograph opposite. The diagram (right) shows the arrangement of the four blocks. The illustrations at the top of the page opposite show the order in which the blocks are joined.

1 SQUARE = 10mm (½in)

S t r i p e d
J e w e l
B o x

Made from scraps of striped silks, this novel and colourful jewel box is large enough to hold all your beads, bracelets and bangles on your dressing table. When not in use, the box can be unbuttoned at the side, opened out and hung on the wall to make an unusual and decorative wallhanging to brighten up your home.

Another project where small offcuts of silk left over from a larger undertaking can be used to great effect, is when the box is simply made from pieces of covered card. The joints are ladder stitched together using silk thread and a fine sewing needle, with the lid hinged with a small strip of silk or held together with a row of tiny ball buttons. The triangular flap is finished off with a hand-made tassel (page 146) worked in a matching shade of embroidery thread.

If you have plenty of plain silk scraps rather than striped ones, cut and stitch strips of these together to make up your own combinations of stripes. Alternatively, use a mixture of striped and patched pieces of fabric.

MATERIALS
- *Pieces of striped silk, at least 20cm (8in) long*
- *20cm (8in) lightweight silk 115cm (45in) wide in a toning colour for lining*
- *20cm (8in) 60g (2oz) polyester wadding 115cm (45in) wide*
- *Silk thread to match the predominating fabric colour, plus a contrasting colour*
- *1 skein pearl cotton embroidery thread for tassel*
- *Tiny ball buttons*
- *Piece of heavy white card 1.2mm–2mm thick*
- *Piece of thin white card 1mm thick*
- *Sharp HB pencil*
- *PVA glue and spreader*
- *Craft knife*
- *Self-healing cutting mat*
- *Ruler*

CUTTING OUT THE CARD AND THE FABRIC

1 Trace off square and triangular templates from page 106. Using the craft knife, cut out six squares and one triangle from the heavy white card to make the box and then the same number from the thin white card for the lining, but this time make the shapes 3mm (¹⁄₈in) smaller all round. Use the heavy card templates to help you cut out the same number of full-size shapes from the wadding.

2 Following the diagram on page 107, place the heavy card templates on the striped fabric and draw round the edge with a sharp HB pencil, making sure the stripes run in the directions indicated on the diagram. Cut out the fabric adding a seam allowance of 1.5cm (⁵⁄₈in) outside the marked lines.

3 Cut out the lining in the same way, but this time use the thin card templates. Add the same seam allowance as for step 2.

QUILTING THE FABRIC

Pin a square of wadding to the wrong side of each piece of fabric, centering it inside the marked lines. Quilt by hand (page 147) or machine (page 45) in random lines using toning and contrasting threads to echo the stripes in the fabric.

MAKING UP THE BOX

1 Lay out the striped squares and triangle on a flat surface with wrong sides facing upwards. Place the heavy card templates over the top, turn over the seam allowance on to the card and either lace (page 106) or glue it in position. Repeat this step with the lining pieces and the thin card templates. Allow the glue to dry thoroughly.

This unusual box is made in striped silk fabric, but you could substitute light- or medium-weight cotton fabric if you prefer. To make a pretty dressing table centrepiece, make up the design in cotton patterned with tiny floral designs, adding clusters of beads or French knots and tiny, applied lace motifs.

2 Make button loops by cutting a strip of silk 2cm × 20cm (³⁄₄in × 8cm) and making it into a rouleau as described on page 145. Cut into six equal pieces. Positioning them as shown in the diagram opposite, sew 5 loops at intervals along the wrong side of edge 1 and one loop on edge 2. Sew on ball buttons to correspond.

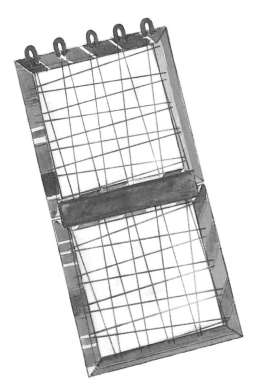

3 Join the edges marked on the diagram with a fabric hinge. Cut a strip of silk 2.5cm (1in) wide and slightly shorter than the length of the box. Fold in half lengthways, turn under the raw edges at each end and slip stitch (page 148) to neaten. Place both edges of the

box together with wrong sides facing and glue the hinge along the edges, leaving a gap of about 2mm (¹⁄₈in) between the edges.

4 Position the lined pieces over the striped pieces with wrong sides facing. Coat the wrong side of the lined piece with glue, allow it to set slightly, then press it on the wrong side of the striped piece. Make sure the edges align, then press the layers under a heavy book while the adhesive sets. Allow to dry thoroughly before proceeding to the next step.

5 Lay the pieces out according to the diagram on page 107 and join the remaining sides with ladder stitch (page 148). Make a tassel (page 146) from the pearl cotton and stitch to the apex of the triangular flap. To use as a wallhanging, make a buttonhole loop at each corner marked 3 on the diagram.

The block for the jewel box is a 13cm (5in) square divided diagonally three times, the flap made from the two smallest triangles. It shows the divisions and directions of the stripes; use it as a piecing diagram.

The letters show where each square should be attached.

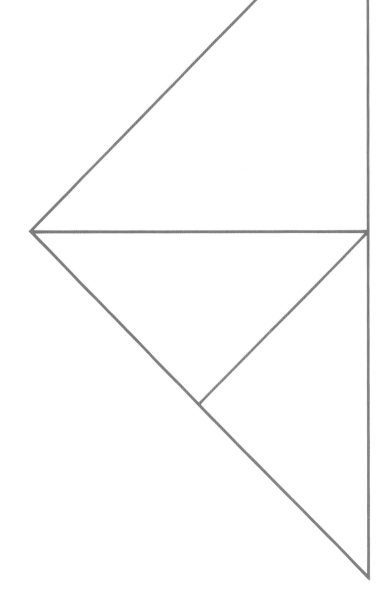

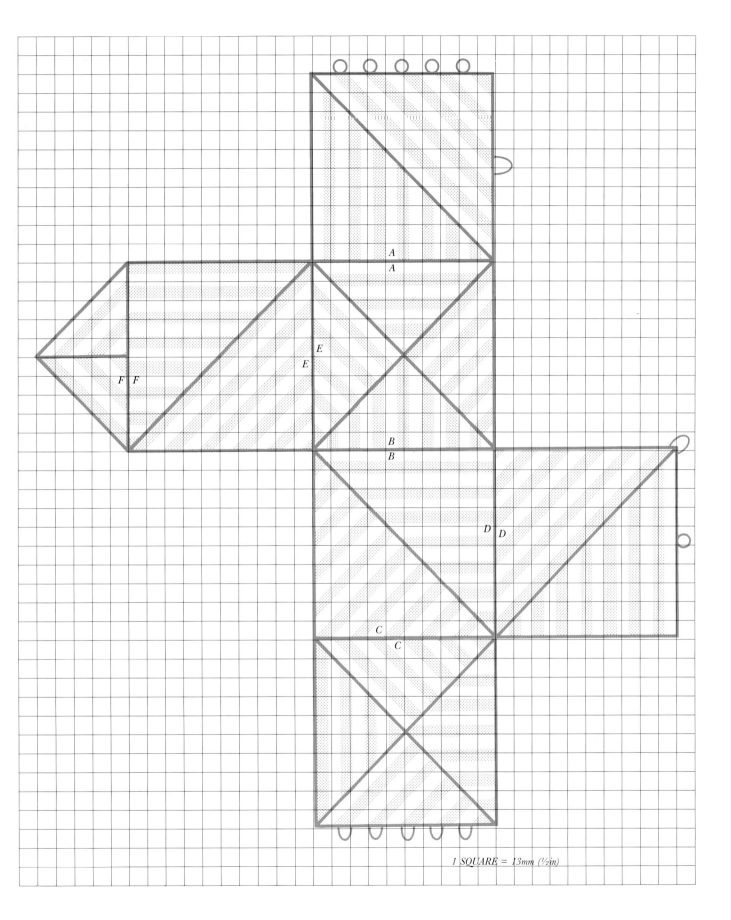

1 SQUARE = 13mm (½in)

Workshop Bag

Log cabin patchwork is a traditional American method of joining rectangular strips of fabric into a block. The technique takes its name from the shape of the walls of a settler's log cabin or barn which, in the old days, were constructed on the ground, then hauled into position around the floor and nailed into place. The centre of the patchwork is traditionally red or black to represent the fire at the heart of the home.

The bag is designed to hold your quilting materials while they are taken to workshops and classes. It will accommodate your cutting board, quilters' ruler, rotary cutter, plus pencils, scissors and other equipment, as well as your pieces of patchwork. The bag has long handles so it can be easily carried over one shoulder, and it ties at the side to keep the contents intact. The inexperienced quilter could make up one large log cabin block about 48cm (19in) square, then fill in the sides with plain fabric to make it up to the correct size. The overall size of the bag is 66cm × 52cm (26in × 20½in) and will take a 62cm × 45cm (24½in × 17¾in) cutting mat.

There are a great many variations on the basic log cabin block and here we show you four different ways in which it can be worked. The rainbow of colours has been chosen so that the coloured strips appear to radiate from the centre of the largest block. When working log cabin patchwork, it is important to keep measuring as you work to be sure that the block remains perfectly square. If you find that any dimensions are not correct, unpick and restitch suspect seams because a slight inaccuracy at this stage will become greater with each added row.

Use cotton fabric for this type of patchwork as it is easy to handle and presses well. A rotary

This workshop bag will soon form an essential part of your equipment when going to a quilting class. The bag holds a cutting board, sketch book and fabric plus quilter's ruler and other tools and is carried on one shoulder, leaving both hands free.

cutter used with a quilters' ruler and self-healing cutting mat will speed up the cutting out process considerably, but take care to cut accurately. Cut away from your body, always closing the guard after every strip. Always press the block after each strip has been machine stitched in position.

There are several simple but effective ways to vary the bag – you might like to add a layer of wadding and quilt the log cabin blocks, for example, or make up a different piece of patchwork using one of the other techniques described in the book. You could also make the back of the bag in a contrasting technique, for example an appliquéd design of pencils and books, or even a miniature quilt.

MATERIALS

- *25cm (10in) of cotton fabric 115cm (45in) wide in 16 colours, graduating from pale yellow through orange, red, purple, blue to green, plus black cut into 32mm × 90cm (1¼in × 36in) strips*
- *60cm (23½in) black cotton fabric 115cm (45in) wide*
- *5cm × 70cm (2in × 27½in) strip of black cotton fabric, pressed in half lengthways*
- *1m (39in) bright yellow cotton fabric 122cm (48in) wide for lining and two pockets*
- *30cm (12in) printed cotton fabric 90cm (36in) wide for small pockets*
- *60cm (24in) black cotton fabric 90cm (36in) wide for back*
- *122cm (48in) red ribbon 2.5cm (1in) wide, cut into four equal pieces*
- *2m (2yds) yellow webbing 2.5cm (1in) wide for the handles, cut into two equal pieces*
- *134cm (53in) wooden dowel 9mm (⅜in) thick, cut into two equal pieces*
- *Sewing thread*
- *Rotary cutter*
- *Self-healing cutting mat*
- *Quilters' ruler*

MAKING THE RADIATING BLOCK

1 Cut one 32mm (1¼in) square from the narrow black strip and one from the pale yellow strip. Pin together with right sides facing and machine stitch along one side, allowing a 6mm (¼in) seam allowance. Press the seam towards the pale yellow square.

2 Turn anti-clockwise so that the pale yellow square is on the left-hand side. Cut a pale yellow strip to fit the top of the yellow/black squares. Pin to the top of the yellow/black squares and stitch. Press as above, then turn anti-clockwise. Cut another pale yellow strip to fit the yellow/black squares. Pin and stitch to the top. Press and turn anti-clockwise.

3 Measure and cut a pale yellow strip to fit the yellow/black/yellow patch. Pin, machine stitch and press as above. This strip finishes the first round, leaving a piece of patched fabric which measures 7cm (2¾in) square.

4 Using the piecing diagram – shown opposite – as a colour guide, continue adding rounds of seven more colours in the same way until you have a block 33.5cm (13¼in) square including seam allowance. Press the block well.

MAKING AND JOINING THE LIGHT AND DARK BLOCKS

1 The next four blocks are smaller and have the coloured strips arranged in pairs as shown in the diagram on page 111. Work in rounds as for the radiating block, changing from light to dark after every second addition, until you have completed three rounds and each block measures 14.5cm (5¾in) square including seam allowance.

2 Arrange two light and dark blocks at each side of the radiating block as shown in the piecing diagram on page 111. Join each pair together with a purple strip, then add another purple strip to the top and the bottom of the pair. Finally, join one pair to each side of the radiating block and press.

MAKING THE DIAGONAL CHEVRON BLOCKS

1 The top left- and right-hand blocks are worked from two sides of the central square only. Cut one 32mm (1¼in) square very carefully from the narrow black strip using small sharp scissors. Join two green strips to adjacent sides of the square, pinning, machine stitching and pressing as previously described.

2 Using the piecing diagram on page 111, continue adding strips to these two sides of the square until you have added six rows and

Log cabin patchwork in its simplest form makes the radiating block at the centre of the bag. More intricate arrangements of colour placing and 'set' are also used. When making this type of patchwork, remember that accuracy and consistency in both cutting and stitching are essential.

each block measures 14.5cm (5¾in) square including seam allowance. Press and leave to one side.

COURTHOUSE STEPS BLOCKS

1 In the final two blocks, a different colour of strip is used on opposite sides of the central square. Cut one 32mm (1¼in) black square. Join one yellow and one orange square of the same size to opposite sides of the black square to make a strip. Measure and cut a turquoise strip and a purple strip to fit along the long sides of the patched strip.

2 Using the piecing diagram on page 111 as a colour guide, continue working in this way until you have completed three rounds and each block measures 14.5cm (5¾in) including seam allowance.

3 Join the blocks together with a pale yellow strip, then join one diagonal chevron block to each side using a purple strip. Press well, then join the top four blocks to the five blocks previously worked and add a purple strip to each side.

4 To finish the front, first add the wider black strip along the top. This will form the channel for the dowel rods. Then add one narrow black strip to the lower edge, then one to each side.

5 Press well all over, then press under a 6mm (¼in) seam allowance along the raw edge of the top band.

ADDING THE LINING AND THE POCKETS

1 From the yellow lining fabric, cut one piece 502mm × 686mm (19¾in × 27in) for the lining and two pieces 470mm × 686mm (18½in × 27in) for the pockets. Cut out pockets to fit your ruler, scissors, rotary cutter and pencils from the printed fabric, allowing an ease of about 12mm (½in) on each side so the equipment will slide into the pockets. Cut out a 686mm × 584mm (27in × 23in) piece of black fabric for the back.

2 Join the back and the front to make the outer bag. Turn under and stitch a narrow hem along the top of the two large yellow pockets, then add the printed pockets to one of these yellow pockets as shown.

MAKING UP THE BAG

1 Lay the bag right side up on a flat surface. Pin ribbons in place at either side, keeping the loose ends away from the sewing line. Place yellow lining under patched front, overlapping slightly at the fold edge. Place the large yellow pocket with added printed pockets right side down on top, again with a slight overlap and place the other yellow pocket over the black back.

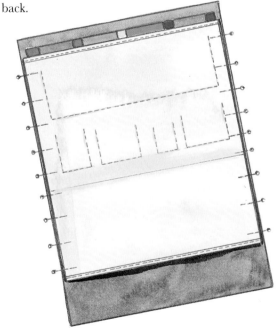

Pin sides then stitch together and turn through to the right side. Turn in the seam at the fold and stitch. Join the back and front.

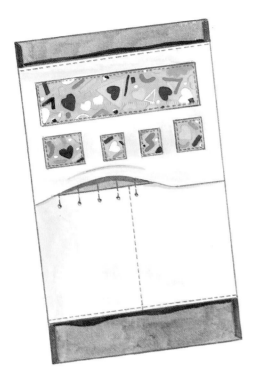

Stitch down the centre of the pocket attached to the back of the bag.

2 Fold over 32mm (1¼in) of black band on the front and the back of the bag, incorporating the webbing handles. Lift the handles above the bag, pin in place and stitch along the fold to secure them. Thread the dowel rod through the channel and slip stitch (page 148) the ends to close.

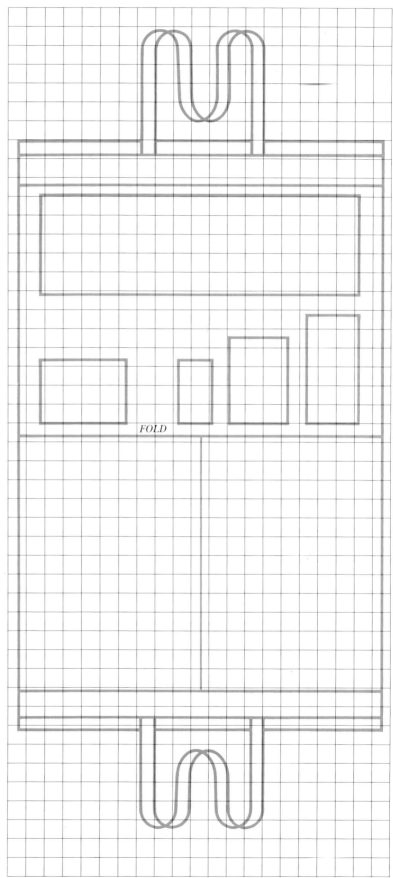

FOLD

One O'Clock Jump

A superbly stitched wholecloth quilt is the jewel in the crown of an experienced quilter and this stylish, queensize example of the craft would make an heirloom to pass down through the family. Named after a famous piece of jazz music, the title also reflects the numerous occasions when the author worked until the early hours to meet the design deadline! The beauty of the evenly worked quilting stitches enhances the design which is based on Odeon-style Art Deco architecture of the nineteen thirties and which breathes new life into an old tradition.

A quilt of this size needs working on a floorstanding frame (page 140). Start quilting at the centre of the design and work gradually outwards until all the main areas have been quilted. Any hard-to-reach areas can be left until the quilt is turned on the frame.

MATERIALS

- *5.5m (6yd) cream cotton fabric 115cm (45in) wide*
- *5.5m (6yd) white cotton backing fabric 115cm (45in) wide*
- *Lightweight wadding to fit a queensize bed*
- *2 reels cream quilting thread in a shade darker than the main fabric*
- *Cream and white sewing thread*
- *10m (10½yd) dressmaker's pattern paper*
- *Quilters' clutch pencil with fine HB leads*
- *Black felt-tipped pen*
- *5cm (2in) wide masking tape*

DRAWING UP THE DESIGN

1 Photocopy the quilt design on page 117. Draw a grid over the design by dividing it half lengthways and widthways, then dividing either side of these lines twice again. This should give you eight divisions along each side and a total of 64 squares on the grid.

2 Join up the dressmakers' pattern paper and draw a rectangle measuring 152cm × 188cm (60in × 74in). Divide this rectangle up in the same way to give you a grid containing 64 squares. Copy the design from the photocopy on to the large grid. Draw the design with a pencil so you can make any alterations easily.
3 Measure out the borders on separate pieces of paper and, using the grid lines as a guide, draw up the border designs. The inner border measures 152cm × 209cm × 10cm (60in × 82in × 4in) and the outer border measures 209cm × 214cm × 20cm (82in × 98in × 8in). When you are happy with all the designs, draw over the pencil lines with the black felt-tipped pen. Attach the border pieces round the edges of the rectangular design to make a full-size design of the complete quilt.

PREPARING THE FABRIC

Measure out the cream top fabric and the white backing, leaving sufficient cream fabric to make the bindings. Remove selvedge edge. You will need to cut and join both fabrics. To do this, cut one width of fabric to the length of the quilt plus seam allowances, then join half a width of fabric at each side of this central panel. Pin, tack and machine stitch the pieces together with matching thread, then press the seams open.

TRANSFERRING THE DESIGN

1 Tack in horizontal and vertical lines on the quilt top so you will be able to align the fabric over the design easily. Lay the full-size design on a flat surface and secure with strips of masking tape. Carefully position the fabric over the top, right side facing upwards, then use masking tape to secure it in place.
2 Check that you have sufficient seam allowance around the edges. Use the clutch pencil to trace the quilting designs on to the fabric, starting at the centre and working outwards and taking care to work accurately and neatly. Draw a fine line right round the edge of the quilt to give you a guide line for positioning the bindings. Draw a line down the centre of the quilt to indicate where the central filling pattern will begin.

Art Deco architecture from the Thirties was the source of the design for this beautiful wholecloth quilt. Although making a quilt of this size requires many hours of painstaking stitching, the sheer pleasure of quilting by hand helps the time to fly. The rows of exquisite quilting complement the geometric design perfectly.

QUILTING THE DESIGN

1 Lay the backing fabric right side down on a flat surface and secure in position with strips of masking tape. Lay the wadding on top, and smooth into position, making sure the wadding reaches to each edge of the backing. Centre the quilt top over the wadding and secure all the layers with pins. Tack the layers together, working outwards from the centre in a grid pattern as shown in the diagram on page 143. Carefully peel off the masking tape.
2 Mount the quilt on a floor-standing quilting frame, following the guide lines on page 140. Quilt (page 147) from the centre, leaving the filling pattern until last. Use strips of 5cm (2in) wide masking tape starting at the centre guide line and working outwards. Quilt the remainder of the design. Don't leave the masking tape in position overnight as the glue may stain the fabric.

MAKING UP THE QUILT

1 Remove the quilt from the frame, remove the tacking stitches and allow the quilt to 'rest' for a couple of days.
2 Cut four binding strips 32mm (1¼in) wide to fit the quilt. Machine stitch the binding in place and slip stitch (page 148) it on the wrong side.
3 Finally make a fabric label (page 8) showing your name, the date and any other information you would like to pass down to future generations. Stitch the label to the back of the quilt.

The border designs for the quilt continue in the order shown on the diagram. The straight filling lines used to quilt background areas are not shown on the diagram – instead, follow the tacked guideline on the quilt and work further lines from the centre outwards to the edge, checking from time to time that the lines remain parallel. On this quilt, the quilted lines are worked 32mm (1¼in) apart, but you may vary this if you prefer.

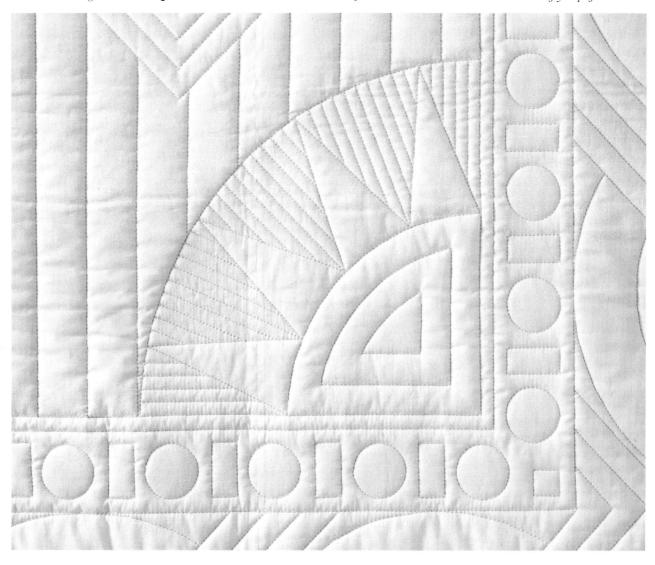

1 SQUARE = 60mm (2½in)

Nursery Animals Playmat

Make this padded playmat to keep your toddler amused while he plays safely on the floor. Eye-catching, stylized animal shapes are applied to squares of brightly coloured plain fabrics. The animals are made from a selection of patterned and textured fabric and they are perfect for small hands to explore new sensations of sight and touch. The playmat comes complete with a pocket containing a miniature teddy bear which can be lifted out by your child and will squeak when it is squeezed.

The playmat is simple to construct and makes an ideal introduction for the beginner to the skills of appliqué, patchwork and quilting, although experienced quilters will also enjoy making up the design. The animals can be laid out in any arrangement you wish and the shapes can be cut out of almost any type of patterned or textured fabric providing it is washable. Your children will enjoy making up names for all of the animals and these can easily be embroidered below the animals using chain stitch (page 149).

To make the project easy for beginners, the animal shapes shown in template form on page 121 have been reversed so they are ready for tracing off, enlarging and transferring to the paper backing of the fusible bonding web. Follow the instructions below and the animals will appear the correct way round on the finished playmat. The final quilting stage is quick to complete as the layers of fabric and wadding are held together with knots of thread rather than lines of stitching. The finished playmat measures 103cm (40½in) square.

The project can be simplified even further by substituting four 48cm (19in) squares of fabric for the 16 smaller squares shown in the photograph. Enlarge the pig, sheep, fish and cat templates on page 121 to fit the larger squares, then apply them and finish off the playmat as described.

MATERIALS

- *30cm (12in) cotton fabric 115cm (45in) wide in blue, yellow and green*
- *60cm (24in) red cotton fabric 115cm (45in) wide*
- *110cm (1¼yd) backing fabric 115cm (45in) wide*
- *Patterned fabric to make four binding strips 104cm × 4cm (41in × 1½in)*
- *110cm (1¼yd) thick polyester wadding 115cm (45in) wide*
- *50cm (20in) fusible bonding web*
- *25cm (10in) pieces of fur fabric, velvet, satin, spotted fabric, striped fabric and gingham*
- *Matching polyester machine threads*
- *Narrow red ribbon*
- *Red rickrack braid*
- *Squeaker*
- *Stranded embroidery thread in dark blue*
- *Crochet cotton*

APPLYING THE ANIMALS

1 Trace off the animal shapes (page 121) enlarge them and transfer to the paper backing of the fusible bonding web, then cut out each shape just outside the traced lines.

2 Using a steam iron set to the correct heat, press the animal shapes on to the wrong side of your chosen fabric. When using pile fabric, place a piece of fur fabric or velvet face up beneath the pile to prevent the pile from being crushed by the iron. Cut out the animal shapes along the traced lines, then peel off the backing paper.

3 Cut out four 24cm (9½in) squares from each colour (red, blue, green, yellow) and one pocket for the teddy bear 28cm × 13cm (11in × 5in). Also cut out four border strips 97cm × 6.5cm (38in × 2½in) from the red fabric.

4 Centre each animal on the appropriate square of fabric and steam press in place, once again using a pad of fur fabric or velvet where necessary to protect the pile. Following the guide lines on page 142, machine zigzag the animals on to the fabric. Outline each shape first, then fill in details such as eyes, the pig's tail and the dog's collar, pull all the front threads through to the back and knot before trimming. If required, embroider names below each animal at this stage, using chain stitch as suggested earlier.

The bright colours and bold animal shapes on this padded playmat will catch and hold a small baby's attention, while an older child will enjoy exploring the different fabric textures. You could also draw up the animal shapes smaller or larger and make simple stencils (page 130) to decorate another project.

MAKING THE TEDDY BEAR

1 Trace off and enlarge the teddy bear template on page 121, adding a seam allowance of 6mm (¼in) all round. Cut out one piece for the front of the bear and one for the back, then draw in the eyes, nose and mouth with a pencil.

2 Place the pieces together with right sides facing and machine stitch round the edge leaving a small gap for stuffing. Press and clip corners (page 151).

3 Carefully turn right side out, using your little finger or a large knitting needle to gently push out the arms, legs and ears. Stuff firmly with toy stuffing or wadding torn into small pieces, remembering to position the squeaker in the bear's tummy. Slip stitch (page 148) the opening closed.

4 Finally, embroider the bear's features in satin stitch (page 149) and running stitch (page 147) and tie a bow of colourful matching narrow ribbon round his neck.

MAKING THE PLAYMAT TOP

1 Lay out the squares on a flat surface. Turn a narrow hem (page 143) along the top of the pocket and sew rickrack braid in place to secure the hem. Place the pocket over the appropriate square and pin it in position, folding a pleat at the centre to accommodate the teddy bear.

2 Using the chain piecing method described on page 144, join the squares to make the quilt top. Press all the seams open. Attach the border pieces, mitre each corner (page 148) and press well.

MAKING UP THE PLAYMAT

1 Lay the backing fabric right side down on a flat surface and secure in position with strips of masking tape. Lay the wadding on top, and smooth into position, making sure the wadding reaches to each edge of the backing.

2 Centre the quilt top over the wadding and secure all the layers with pins, working outwards from the centre in a grid pattern as shown in the diagram on page 148. Carefully peel off the masking tape. Large glass-headed pins are useful as they will hold the wadding.

3 To make the ties, thread your needle with a double length of crochet cotton, then make a double stitch (page 98) through all the layers where the corners of four squares meet. Tie a reef knot (page 151) on the back with the thread ends, then trim them to 2.5cm (1in) long and secure the knot with a small dab of fabric glue. Repeat the stitching and tying sequence across the quilt at each point where four corners meet.

4 Bind the edges of the quilt, following the illustrated instructions on page 143, and slip the teddy bear into the pocket. You may like to finish off the quilt with a personalized fabric label bearing the child's name, date of birth and your own name embroidered in back stitch (page 149) or satin (page 149) on one of the plain squares.

The animal shapes are shown here in reverse so they can be enlarged and traced directly on to fusible bonding web. The animals will then appear the correct way round on the finished mat.

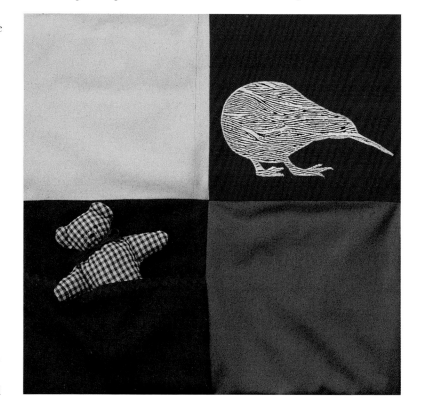

Quilted Cushion Cover

Make this delicate rainbow cushion cover to practice your quilting skills on the sewing machine. The quilting, carried out in buttonhole thread, forms an attractive geometric design on the cushion and is quite easy to work, providing you are accurate when stitching and keep the stitched lines perfectly straight and even. The cushion cover will fit a 28cm (11in) cushion pad and the back of the cover is made from plain white fabric.

The tiny matching humbug-shaped cushion is actually a pot pourri sachet and measures 10cm (4in) across. Stuff the sachet with polyester stuffing to which you have added pot pourri.

MATERIALS
- *40cm (16in) lightweight white cotton fabric 115cm (45in) wide*
- *40cm (16in) thin wadding or needlepunch (loomtex) wadding 115cm (45in) wide*
- *40cm (16in) muslin backing fabric 115cm (45in) wide*
- *130cm (51in) multicoloured cord*
- *Buttonhole thread in red, orange, yellow, green, blue, purple*
- *Size 90 (14) machine needle for use with buttonhole thread*
- *White polyester machine thread for bobbin*
- *28cm (11in) cushion pad*
- *28cm (11in) white zip fastener*
- *Polyester stuffing*
- *Dried lavender, rose petals or mixed pot pourri*
- *Sharp HB pencil*

A thick buttonhole thread was used to machine quilt this delightful cushion. A finer machine thread will produce a more delicate effect, or you could work the design in a self-coloured thread to create an interesting textural pattern.

MAKING THE CUSHION FRONT

1 Cut out a square 33cm (13in) from the white fabric, wadding and muslin backing, plus two pieces 31cm × 20cm (12in × 8in) for the back of the cover. (The front of the pillow will shrink slightly due to the quilting.)

2 Trace off the design on page 125 and enlarge it to the required size as shown on page 141. Lay the white cotton over your tracing and secure it in place with strips of masking tape. Draw over each line with a sharp HB pencil. These lines mark the lines of quilting on the cushion.

3 Assemble and tack the layers of fabric, wadding and backing together as shown on page 143. Using the machine foot as a guide, stitch along the lines marked blue on the diagram, starting from the centre. Repeat with the other thread colours until the quilted design is complete.

MAKING UP THE CUSHION

Pin out the front on your ironing board and leave it to settle. Run a line of tacking round the cushion front to mark out an area 30cm (12in) square. This is the finished size of the cushion. To make up the cushion cover, follow the illustrated instructions on page 145, using the tacked line as a stitching guide. Finally, slip stitch (page 148) the cord round the cover, turning in the ends neatly.

MAKING THE POT POURRI SACHET

Cut out a piece of white cotton 28cm × 11.5cm (11in × 4½in) and a piece of needlepunch (loomtex) wadding the same size. Pin the fabric and wadding together and tack as shown on page 143. Work the quilted design on page 124 in the same way as the cushion cover (above).

2 Join A to A. Fold in centre and join B to B. Open C edge and fold to form humbug. Half sew, then turn through, stuff and close opening. Stuff with a mixture of wadding and pot pourri. Ladder stitch (page 148) the opening closed.

Transfer the main guidelines on to the fabric, then use the edge of your machine foot to indicate the position of the other lines. Take care to leave the needle in the 'down' position when you change the direction of the stitching. Work six or seven rows in each thread colour.

The illustrations below and opposite show where the areas of colour fall. The gaps between will vary according to the width of the sewing machine foot.

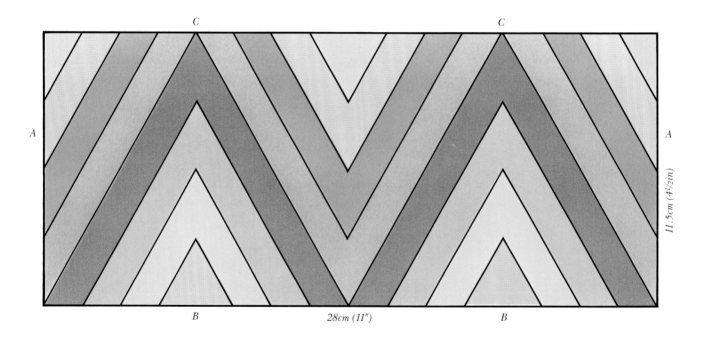

C   C

A   A

11.5cm (4½in)

B   *28cm (11")*   B

Child's Sashiko Jacket

Make this quilted jacket to keep a small child snug and warm. Sashiko, a traditional Japanese quilting technique can be worked with or without wadding behind the fabric, and it uses a contrasting thread on a plain background. The bold outline designs are worked in a thick thread so the stitches stand out well from the background. The design on this jacket uses traditional Japanese patterns and follows the oriental taste for asymmetrical shapes.

Buy a commercial paper pattern for a child's simple jacket with raglan sleeves and a patch pocket. Follow the making-up instructions supplied with the pattern in conjunction with the quilting instructions below.

MATERIALS
- Red cotton fabric and lining as specified on your paper pattern
- 25cm (10in) lightweight non-woven interfacing 90cm (36in) wide
- White coton à broder embroidery thread
- Buttons
- Dressmakers' carbon paper
- Heavyweight tracing paper
- Old, dry ballpoint pen
- Masking tape

PREPARING THE FABRIC
1 Cut the pattern pieces out of the red fabric and the lining. Join the sleeves to the fronts of the jacket, pressing seams open and snipping into them so they lie flat.

The jacket features traditional Japanese quilting designs worked in a thick, strongly contrasting thread. Stitches for Sashiko quilting are evenly spaced but slightly larger than those used in European quilting.

2 Trace off the Sashiko motifs and enlarge from page 129, making a length of at least 63cm (25in) for the ocean design and 30cm (12in) for the hemp flower design. Press in the seam allowance down the jacket fronts and overlap the fronts, tacking them together.

3 Using the diagram as a guide, place the tracings on the jacket and hold in position with masking tape. Check the diagonal design matches across both fronts. Slip a piece of dressmakers' carbon paper underneath the tracings, then transfer the designs by pressing along the lines with the dry ballpoint pen. Transfer the designs on to the pocket, fronts, sleeves, edges and back of the jacket.

4 Cut out pieces of non-woven interfacing slightly larger than the transferred designs and tack them onto the wrong side of the fabric. This will help the stitched designs to 'sit' well on the fabric.

QUILTING THE JACKET
Work small running stitches (page 147) along the design lines using the white embroidery thread. Work evenly spaced stitches along the long lines first, then 'float' the needle across the wrong side of the fabric and join up the smaller shapes.

MAKING UP THE JACKET
When all the quilted designs are complete, carefully trim down the surplus interfacing on the wrong side. Make up and line the jacket following the pattern instructions.

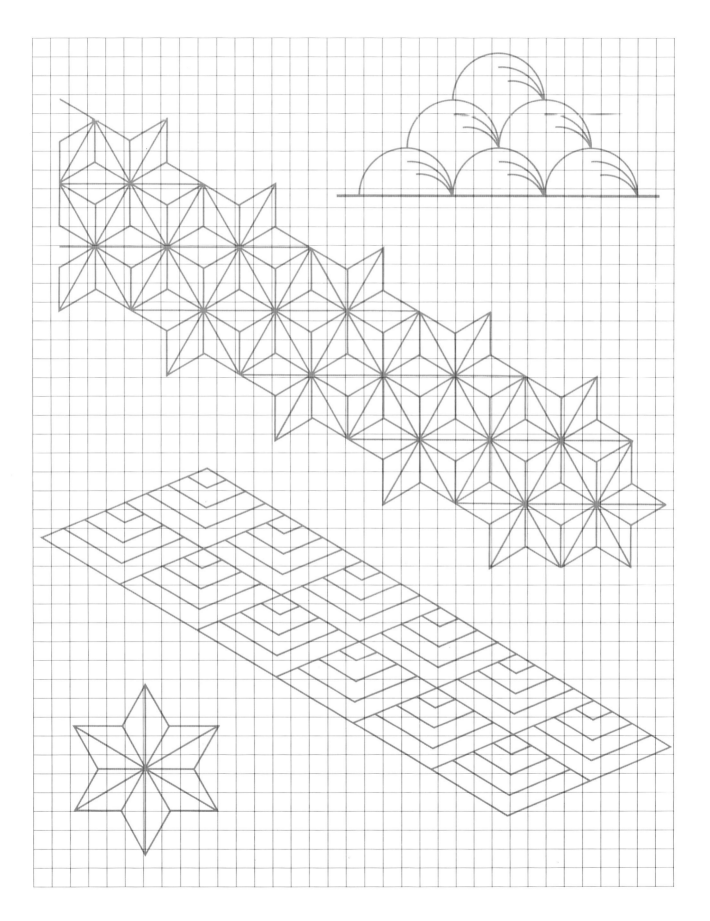

1 SQUARE = 10mm (½in)

Starry, Starry Night

A midnight blue velvet waistcoat is embellished with stencilled gold stars, sequins, quilted shooting star trails and a striking gold lamé lining.

Use a commercial paper pattern for your waistcoat, choosing one which has no darts or panels, and take care to cut the front pieces out so that the pile of the velvet lies in the same direction on each one. Always press velvet face down on a special pressing board or on a spare piece of velvet to avoid crushing the pile.

MATERIALS

- *Blue cotton velvet and gold lamé for the lining as specified on your paper pattern*
- *90cm (1yd) needlepunch (loomtex) wadding*
- *Blue polyester sewing thread for the velvet*
- *White polyester sewing thread for the lamé*
- *Silk sewing thread for tacking*
- *Yellow or gold quilting thread*
- *Tiny gold beads*
- *Star sequins*
- *Buttons as specified on your paper pattern*
- *Can of gold spray paint suitable for craft use*
- *Stencil card*

DECORATING THE FRONTS

1 Cut out two fronts separately from the velvet, making sure the pile runs in the same direction on each piece and that you have one left and one right front. Also cut two front shapes from the wadding. Lay the velvet pieces on a flat surface with the right sides facing upwards.

2 Decide where to place the stencilled stars and mark the centre of each star with a pin. Trace off the star template and cut out from the stencil card. Stick pieces of double-sided tape to the back and remove protective paper. Cover the fronts with newspaper, position the stencil over a pin, then check that there is no fabric showing except where you want a star.

3 Remove the pin, shake and spray the gold paint on the stencil. Allow each star shape to dry thoroughly before moving the newspaper. This can be a long process when spraying several stars, but it is essential to let the paint dry to avoid smudges.

4 Tack the fronts to the wadding with the silk thread so that no marks will be left in the pile. Sew a gold bead on each star point. Mark the position of the shapes of each shooting star trail between the stencilled stars with a pin. Quilt (page 147) the shooting star trails, then add beads and a star sequin to each trail.

MAKING UP THE WAISTCOAT

Cut out the back and the lining from the lamé. Make up and line the waistcoat following the pattern instructions, taking care to work the buttonholes neatly. If your sewing machine has a 'walking' foot, use it when sewing the velvet.

Make this festive waistcoat in luxurious velvet or a heavyweight cotton or silk fabric to wear when celebrating a special occasion. Add the finishing touch with a bow tie made from lighter weight fabric in a co-ordinating colour.

Wish You Were Here

This appliquéd scene inspired by a picture-postcard Greek village invites you to sit with a glass of ouzo and watch the world go by, thinking of your happy memories of sun, leisure and holidays. The village and boat are constructed separately on a white fabric base, using fusible bonding web, then added together with the hills, sea and trees to the lightly-speckled background.

MATERIALS

- *50cm (½yd) white cotton fabric 115cm (45in) wide*
- *60cm (24in) speckled cotton background fabric 115cm (45in) wide*
- *30cm (12in) cotton fabric 115cm (45in) wide in blue and three shades of green for the sky and hills*
- *30cm (12in) cotton fabric 115cm (45in) wide in blue and turquoise for the sea*
- *2m (2yds) fusible bonding web*
- *Scraps of white fabric*
- *Scraps of striped yellow, red and pale blue fabric*
- *Short length of cord*
- *Fabric for binding or border*
- *Firm non-woven interfacing for backing*
- *Small turquoise beads*
- *Selection of polyester or machine embroidery threads*
- *Soft pencil and 2 battens to fit width of picture*

PREPARING THE FABRIC

1 The design is shown on page 135 so that it can be easily traced off on to the bonding web. Enlarge the design, using the grid method shown on page 141, to 94cm × 36cm (37in × 14in). Use this as your master design and also as a fabric key.

2 Trace the village, hills, sky, boat and steps on to bonding web. Cut a piece of white fabric 30cm × 94cm (12in × 37in) and trace

This imaginative fabric picture depicting a tranquil village and harbour scene in Greece is made using fusible bonding web and machine satin stitch.

the outline of the village on to it using a soft pencil. Trace guide lines for the hills, harbour, boat, steps and pavement on to the speckled background fabric.

3 Cut a piece of white fabric 36cm × 13cm (14in × 5in) for the boat base. Select fabrics for the houses, tavernas, church, awnings, hills, boats, steps and bollards and apply bonding web shapes to the wrong side. Stick tiny pieces of your chosen fabric on to the design to make a key. Apply a strip of bonding web about 15cm (6in) to the wrong side of each of the blue and turquoise sea fabrics. Cut out wave shapes.

ASSEMBLING THE PICTURE

1 Apply the house shapes to the white fabric and join them with machine satin stitch. Add windows, doors and awnings. Stitch the window boxes with a wide, random zigzag stitch in several shades of green, red and pink. Stitch the small windows and balconies with machine satin stitch. Shade the sides of the buildings with straight machine stitching. Fill in all the details and trim to size.

2 Make up the boat on a separate piece of fabric and trim to size. Apply the sea on to the background fabric, outlining the waves with satin stitch, following the harbourside guide lines and leaving a gap for the boat, pavement and steps.

3 Apply the hills to the background fabric and then tack the village in place on the background and outline with satin stitch.

Work the crosses on the church in gold thread. Apply the boat, bollards and steps and add a piece of cord to anchor the boat to the bollards. Stitch on tiny beads to give sparkle to the sea.

4 Make the trees and plants from tiny pieces of fabric mixed with scraps of peeled bonding

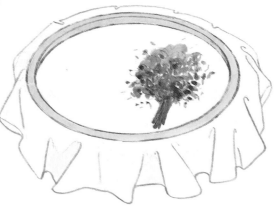

web. Lay the scraps in the desired position on the picture, cover with a piece of backing paper from the bonding web, then press carefully to bond the pieces together. Secure with a few wide zigzag stitches.

FINISHING THE PICTURE

There are two ways of finishing the picture. You can back it with interfacing and bind the edges or add a border with mitred corners (page 144). Attach sleeves (page 150) at the top and bottom on the back to accommodate battens.

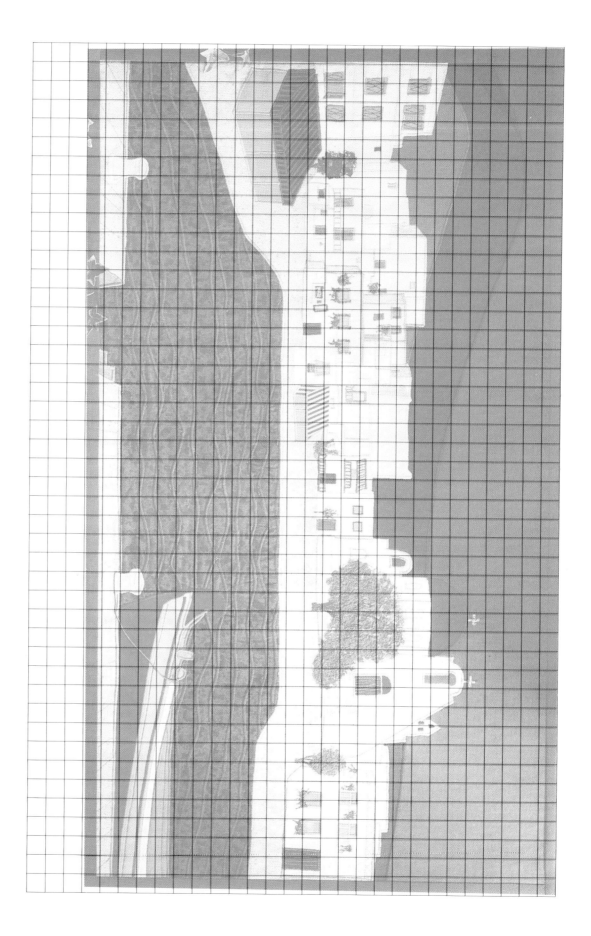

1 SQUARE = 21mm

EQUIPMENT AND TECHNIQUES

Patchwork, quilting and appliqué are crafts which can be taken up without the necessity to buy expensive equipment. However, as the crafts have become more and more popular over the last 15 years or so, many useful aids have been developed to speed up and improve accuracy during the repetitive part of marking up, cutting and piecing. A visit to a specialist quilt shop will reveal a treasure trove of tools.

Equipment

After you have patched, quilted or appliquéd your first project and are hooked on the subject, you will want to extend your range of equipment by collecting the following items:

Scissors: To start with, buy a good pair of dressmaker's scissors and keep them only for cutting fabric, a medium-sized pair for paper and small sharp scissors for close work. I also have a small pair of scissors with the tips of the blades broken off which I use to cut thread when I'm quilting so there is less chance of accidentally snipping the quilt top.

Pins and threads: Good quality pins and needles are important too, so that the fabric does not snag. The best needle to use for both hand sewing and quilting is a between, as it is short and easy to handle. Medium grey and cream threads are ideal for patchwork as the colours blend with multi-patterned materials and this can help to hide stitches. When you are working by hand, use cotton thread on cotton fabric, but a thread made from a mixture of polyester and cotton has a slight stretch which works well on the sewing machine and does not melt when pressed.

Collect together a steam iron, sharp pencil, eraser, sheets of dressmaker's pattern paper and card and you are ready to go!

Paper: Squared paper in metric or imperial divisions and isometric graph paper are used for working out blocks or the complete quilt. Buy tracing paper in various weights and use the heavier weights for quilting designs. Dressmakers' pattern paper and dressmakers' carbon paper are useful. Make templates from medium-weight card or use template plastic, which can be printed with a grid. Template plastic, which can be cut with scissors (take care to use your paper pair for this, not the fabric ones), lasts longer than card, and because it is semi-transparent, it allows you to trace from books and centre a motif on printed fabric.

Templates: Ready-made templates can be purchased in metal or plastic. They usually include a 6mm ($\frac{1}{4}$in) seam allowance and they are sometimes made in two pieces so that a motif may be centred through the 'window' portion.

Pencil box: Buy a pencil box and fill it with the following items: a good quality pencil sharpener, a soft eraser, coloured pencils, both hard and soft grades of lead pencil, a quilter's clutch pencil with fine leads for marking fabric. Also buy a black felt-tipped pen for thickening design lines, and purchase silver, gold or yellow pencils for marking dark fabrics.

Drafting: There is an extensive range of measuring aids, but the plastic quilter's rule has measurements that can be used for mitring too. Use it with a rotary cutter on a self-healing cutting mat. You will also need a metre (yard) measuring stick; some builders' merchants have longer plastic rulers which are useful when working on large projects. Specialist quilters' shops can supply triangle or square rules and two implements for marking 6mm ($\frac{1}{4}$in) seam allowances – a brass seam marker for curves or a quarter seamer for straight lines.

A large set square is vital to help keep corners square and you will also need a steel rule or straight-edge plus a craft knife with sharp blades. Always work with a sharp blade to avoid accidents. When working with curved shapes you will need a compass and a protractor. I also have a long metal rule 12mm ($\frac{1}{2}$in) wide with holes drilled through at 12mm ($\frac{1}{2}$in) intervals. By holding this down with a pin at one end and a pencil in the desired hole, I use it to draw circles. Larger circles are made with a pin, string, pencil and my husband as this occupation needs two people. The ruler was made for me by a friend who also made me a special metal rule 32mm ($1\frac{1}{4}$in) wide for measuring bias strips.

Miscellaneous items: Masking tape in various widths is used as quilting guides and you should always hold down the paper on which you are designing with a piece of masking tape in each corner. It will not slip around and your measurements will be much more accurate! Stationers' dots have many uses – identifying plastic templates, blocks, cut-up fabric, the wrong and right sides of templates. Pieces of double-sided tape can be used on the back of templates and rulers help stop them slipping on fabric. Fabric glue and liquid fray-check, which is

Below, using mirror tiles to reflect images, and using croppers to isolate parts of a patterned fabric.

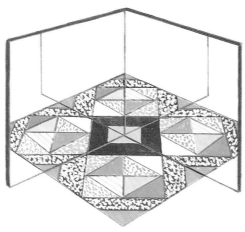

painted on cut fabric edges to prevent fraying, are also useful. Two mirror tiles, taped together at right angles with carpet tape, will reflect four images. A reducing glass, available from specialist quilter's supply shops, will let you view your design in miniature and help you to judge the effect. It is also useful when choosing patterned fabrics to see the effect one pattern has on another. Make some croppers out of shaped black card following the diagram. Make pairs in

several sizes as these are invaluable for isolating elements on patterned material. Try to find a drawer or large box to keep all these items together as this will save time and temper when you start designing.

The workbox: Needles come in sizes from 5 to 12, with size 12 being the finest. Each type has a particular use, but a useful phrase to remember

is 'small needles, small stitches'. Buy good quality needles and if they develop a snag on the tip, throw them away. Straws (or milliners' needles) are long and useful for tacking, especially when stitching through wadding. Sharps are used for general sewing and dressmaking, while betweens are the best for quilting. A bodkin is a thick, blunt needle used for turning rouleaux and threading elastic. Buy fine pins made from steel so that they do not rust when left in fabric. Glass-headed pins are good when pinning wadding and small safety pins can sometimes be used instead of tacking. Also buy a good quality tape measure with measurements on both sides.

Thread: Use special cotton tacking thread rather than leftover sewing threads when tacking. Tacking thread is not polished so the hairy finish sticks to the fabric weave and holds well. If you have sewn through tacking thread, it will snap easily rather than pulling a stitch out. Use silk thread to tack silk, velvet or satin so that no marks are left behind. Cotton thread is good for handsewing cotton fabrics, but puckers polyester/cotton blend fabrics when used on the sewing machine. Polyester-covered cotton thread works with most fabrics, whether stitched by hand or by machine. Choose a slightly darker tone if you are not able to match a colour exactly. Hand quilting thread, a strong cotton or polyester/cotton mixture is available prewaxed, but if using the unwaxed type, run each length of thread through a cake of beeswax. This strengthens the thread and helps to prevent knotting. Silk thread should be used on silk in order to prevent wear and tear nylon thread is good for machine quilting where a colour would be intrusive. Use metallic and lurex machine threads and hand embroidery threads to work details and textures.

Thimbles: These can be a prickly subject. Wherever quilters gather, you will see sore fingers being compared. The lucky quilters learned to use a thimble when they were young, but it's hard to start later in life. I suspect part of the trouble is getting a comfortable fit and I would compare the search for the perfect thimble to buying shoes – it takes time. Visit a jeweller where there might be some secondhand silver thimbles that have been worn into a slightly oval shape. A jeweller can repair worn thimble tops and you might find that you have unwittingly started a collection as friends and relatives rally round with offerings. There are various types of thimble, metal, plastic, leather, open top – but I favour a metal thimble without a pronounced ridge round the base.

Sewing machine: It's as important as your right arm, so get to know it well. A simple hand machine will sew cotton patchwork beautifully, but if you intend to use polyester/cotton blends, satin, lurex, silk or knitted fabrics, you will need a swing needle machine, in other words, one that will do zigzag stitching. A simple machine from a local specialist shop with a good reputation is usually the best choice unless you intend to do a lot of decorative work. There is less to go wrong and you can spend the money you have saved on fabric. Sewing machine needles comes in various sizes, but size 80 is a good size for most purposes. Needles need to be changed frequently – sewing synthetic fabrics and machining over pins blunts them quickly.

Iron and boards: A steam iron will make good crisp seams. Take care that your ironing board is high enough not to give you backache. Mine is broad and I often use it as an extra worktable. You can put a piece of board across the top to enlarge it. A sandpaper board, made from the finest grade sandpaper glued to heavy cardboard, holds small pieces of fabric steady when tracing round templates. It also helps you to draw a fine, clear line on the fabric.

Softboard or wall panel: A wall covered in soft insulating board painted white will enable you to hang up your work, stand back from it and judge how the patterns, colours, secondary designs are working. It's useful for pinning work on to while taking photographs at various stages of construction, perhaps to test the 'set' of blocks. Large polystyrene panels or tiles are useful too to pin your work on to and keep it crease-free.

Camera: A camera is essential, for once you start visiting quilt shows you will want to make visual notes. As you become more observant and notice design interpretations it can also be used to record architecture, floral arrangements, landscapes and other potential design sources. A suitable easy-to-use camera is a 35mm compact, with zoom lens for close-up details, built-in flash

and an over-ride facility. Make sure the model you choose will allow you to get close up to the work. Some models have a macro or close focusing capability, which is useful for details. Lighting in public places ranges from very warm tungsten to green fluorescent. Daylight filtering through a marquee gives a particularly unpleasant yellow cast. To deal with this you need to switch on your camera flash, even when the built-in meter shows that there is sufficient ambient light to take the shot.

Camera flash units are a neutral light source, but sometimes will bleach out the centre of the picture. Make yourself familiar with your camera; stand up straight with your elbows close to your body and use the viewfinder frame. Many photographs are spoiled by camera shake, so always be sure to take your time and think through what you are framing. Read the manual carefully several times and learn how to judge how far you are standing from your subject.

Quilting frames: Although it is quite possible to quilt while holding the fabric in your hand, a frame will keep both it and the stitches smoother. There are circular and oval quilting frames which can be held in the hand or attached to floor stands, often incorporating a work light. Freestanding full-sized frames come in tubular plastic and wood, the latter in both off-the-peg and made-to-measure styles. Their great advantages are that the work remains clean, uncrumpled and instantly accessible and several quilters can work on one piece together. Most freestanding frames can be dismantled for storage.

Light box: There are various types of light box sold in craft and art supplies shops. A light box is useful when transferring designs, but you can achieve almost the same effect, at a fraction of the price, by placing a lamp under a glass-topped coffee table and covering the top with a sheet of tracing paper to diffuse the light. For large pieces of work, tape both drawing and fabric to a window to transfer the design.

An old chair with a removable seat can also be used. Place the glass from a clip picture frame (this has the edges ground smooth) on the chair. Cover with a sheet of tracing paper and put a lamp underneath, shining upwards.

Essential techniques

ENLARGING A DESIGN

Enlarging a design to the correct size is quite simple to do, but remember that accurate measuring is important. Divide up the original design with a grid into squares of equal size, then carefully copy the design, square for square, onto a larger grid of the required size.

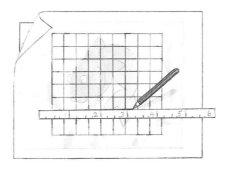

1 First, trace the design on to tracing paper. Draw a grid over the tracing and then draw in a diagonal line from bottom left to top right, as shown. Using the diagonal line as a guide, draw a larger grid containing the same number of squares on separate paper.

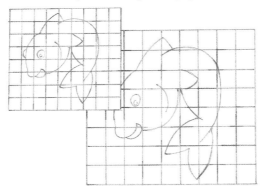

2 Copy the design by marking the larger grid at each place where the design crosses the original grids then join up these marks. Once the complete design has been transferred onto the larger grid, check it back very carefully against the original.

REDUCING A DESIGN

To make a design smaller, follow the steps above, but this time transpose the design on to a smaller grid of the required size.

DRAWING A LARGE CIRCLE

This method is useful when you do not have a compass with an extension bar. Tie a pencil at the end of a length of fine string. Tie a knot at the other end, then pin this end down on a piece of paper laid on a flat surface and secured with masking tape. Holding the pencil upright, draw a circle on the paper. A tried and tested method for drawing varying degrees of circle sizes, is to adjust the length of the string to different lengths. To draw a large circle increase the length of string, to reduce it, shorten the string.

TRANSFERING QUILT DESIGNS

Commercial plastic stencils come in a wonderful variety of designs and they are simple to use – you simply place a pencil in the cut-out slots and draw the design. Printed designs can be traced over directly on to fabric, using a light box or window (page 141). Card or plastic template material will make simple shapes to draw round. Quilting designs can be drawn on thick tracing paper with a felt-tipped pen. The tracing is then placed over a sheet of dressmaker's carbon laid over the fabric, and a spiked tracing wheel is drawn over the design lines and this transfers them on to the fabric as lines of dots. Self-adhesive plastic cut to shape may be stuck directly on to the quilt top as a guide to quilt around, rather in the same way as strips of masking tape.

The marking should be done with great care. Use a quilter's clutch pencil with a fine lead for marking light fabrics and a yellow, silver or gold pencil for dark ones. Keep coloured pencils sharpened to make a fine line. It is also possible to use tailor's chalk if you are marking a design as you go along, or you can make a line with a sliver of soap. A soap line leaves no marks behind. There are a few specialist marking pens containing special inks which either fade when exposed to air or can be sponged off with water. Although these are quick and easy to use, the long term effect of the chemicals is not known.

A FLOOR-STANDING QUILTING FRAME

Pin or tack the quilt to the webbing strips attached to the lengthways runners, making sure that the sides are parallel. It's always a good idea to use a larger piece of backing fabric or pin on extra strips of fabric round the sides so you can attach the quilt to the frame without causing damage. Roll the quilt on to the runners and tighten the tensioning devices. Support the side edges by pinning a piece of tape to the quilt and passing it around the side bars.

It is a matter of personal preference whether you quilt with the top held taut or loose. Always loosen off the tension and cover the quilt with a clean sheet when you finish each quilting session. Keep all the tools you need including thread and scissors in a little basket placed close to the frame so that they are always on hand.

FABRIC GRAIN

The terms 'grain' or 'straight grain' refer to the weave from top to bottom of a piece of fabric (the warp) and from side to side (the weft). Try stretching a piece of cotton from side to side, then stretch it from top to bottom. You will see that it is fairly firm. Now try stretching it from the top right-hand corner to the bottom left-hand corner and observe the stretch. This is the true cross (bias). It is helpful to construct blocks so the sides are cut on the straight grain so that they do not stretch and become longer, causing inaccuracies when piecing. On the other hand, curves will be smoother and easier to handle if they are cut on the bias. Always mark the straight grain line on templates.

Just to make life more difficult, however, fabric is often printed 'off grain' at the factory. When a particular pattern is important to the overall design of a quilt, it may be necessary to adjust the grain line. An off-grain print can sometimes be corrected by dampening the fabric and tugging it straight. This process requires two people.

Sometimes a fabric will catch the light in a different way when cut across or down the weave. Velvet and needlecords (corduroy) which have a pile and satin are good examples, but this effect can also occur on cotton. It's very hard to spot when cutting out, but when patched the difference will show up.

MACHINE STITCHING

Always work a practice piece before starting to machine stitch or machine quilt a project to check that the thread, needle and stitch size and fabric are compatible. Fit a new needle before starting to sew as a blunt one will damage the fabric and result in uneven stitching.

MACHINE APPLIQUÉ

Insert a new needle and set your machine to a close zigzag stitch about 2½ wide on the width of stitch dial. Use a special appliqué foot if one is provided with your machine. Test the stitch on a spare piece of fabric, practising points and corners, and adjust the machine as necessary. Begin stitching at the beginning of a straight edge and don't go too fast. When working intricate shapes, turn the wheel by hand to make one stitch at a time, pivot at the corners by leaving the needle in the fabric, raising the presser foot and turning the fabric before lowering the foot and continuing to stitch. Never turn the wheel of the machine backwards as this will cause damage.

SEAM ALLOWANCES

Seam allowances are generally 6mm (¼in) wide. On fabrics which fray badly it's wise to make the allowance a little wider. The seam allowance can either be pressed open or to one side. Sometimes you will need to press to one side to avoid the seam allowance showing through a pale fabric. This will make quilting easier on one side than the other and produce a slight ridge.

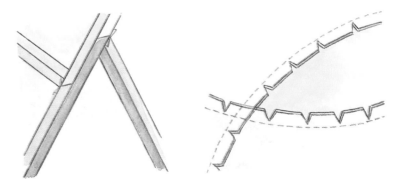

SEAMS

A flat seam pressed open will give a more uniform surface and it can be quilted on either side of the seam line or 'in the ditch' (page 46) where the stitches will be hidden within the join. Curved seams are usually pressed towards the inside edge of the curve, but if this causes bulk, they may be pressed the other way. Where you have several seams in the same place, layer them by trimming each one to a different width.

CHAIN PIECING

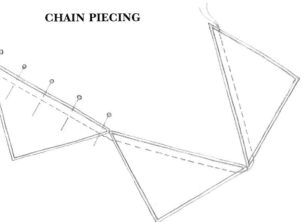

Unless you are working on tight curves or areas where it is important that points should meet up, it is not always necessary to tack patchwork. Instead, insert pins horizontally, making sure that the two pieces of fabric are correctly aligned. Pass the patches under the machine needle, one after the other, letting the machine run for a moment in between to make a 'chain' of thread. Check each piece before pressing and correct the seam where necessary.

TACKING FOR APPLIQUE

Hand appliqué always needs to be tacked, unless you are using the freezer paper technique (page 51). Machine appliqué need only be tacked when fusible bonding web is not being used.

TACKING FOR QUILTING

Tacking the quilt top before quilting is very important, in order that the layers of fabric and wadding will not slip and pucker. I tack in rows about 6cm (2½in) apart. Prepare for tacking by pressing the backing fabric and placing it face down on a flat surface. Hold the edges in place with masking tape or drawing board clips. Lay the wadding over the backing fabric and centre it, making sure that the wadding covers all the fabric edges. Place the pressed quilt top on the

wadding with the right side facing upwards. Check that all the sides match and fit, then pin across and down the centre of the quilt. Tack from the centre outwards, gently smoothing excess fabric to the edges gently as you work. Work plenty of rows of tacking so that there will be no movement during quilting (Tacking stitch page 148).

BINDINGS AND EDGES

As quilt edges are often straight, it is not usually necessary to cut binding on the bias, but scalloped edges will need bias-cut binding. Binding

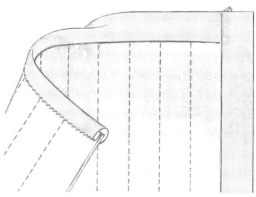

is usually attached from the front of the quilt and slip stitched (page 148) to the back. Binding can, however, be mitred in the same way as a border (page 144). Another method of finishing the edges is to cut the backing fabric large enough to roll the edges round and slip stitch them to the front. This technique can be worked the other way round by cutting a larger top piece and slip stitching the edges down on the back. Extra

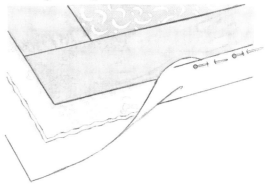

stuffing can be inserted inside this type of finish and a line of quilting will finish the edge neatly. The edge of a quilt takes a lot of hard wear, so purchased bias binding is not suitable, unless it is cut from good quality cotton. Not all quilts have binding round the edges. Instead, the top layer of fabric is folded in around the wadding, then the backing fabric is also folded in and the quilting holds the raw edges neatly together.

Fancy edges may also be inserted round the outside of a quilt, such as curves, piping, prairie points or some part of a motif from the main quilt. Asymmetrical edges are becoming more popular as quilters experiment by making their designs break out of the normal square or rectangular shape. Large 'escapes' may need some form of support and careful hanging.

MITRING CORNERS ON BORDERS

1 Pinch-mark the centres of the quilt top and two opposite border pieces. Matching the marks, pin with right sides together. Tack and machine stitch, beginning and ending 6mm (¼in) short of the end of the quilt. Join the remaining two borders in the same way and press flat. One border will overlap the adjacent one at right angles of each corner.

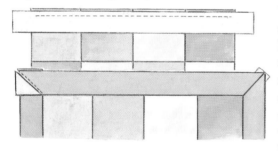

2 Fold under the top border piece to make a 45° angle running from the inner to the outer edge. Pin together from the wrong side and stitch from the quilt side outwards. Trim away surplus fabric and press the seam open. Repeat for the remaining three corners.

BACKING FABRIC

Backing fabric is a poor relation to the front of the quilt when a cheap fabric is used. In fact, attractive backing for a quilt can make a wonderful surprise, whether it has been patched specially or features an exciting fabric. Patched backs often come about because there is not quite enough fabric. Always make the backing at least 5cm (2in) wider all round than the top.

BORDERS

The border is, in some ways, the most important aspect of a quilt whether it is divided into several widths using both plain and patterned fabric, patched or densely quilted. The border is the frame round the main design, so it can pick up colours from the design or it can be a narrow binding in a contrasting fabric.

Ideally, measurements taken from the initial quilt design should be used when cutting a border, but in practice patched fabric often stretches and the initial measurements may not be correct. Care needs to be taken, however, not to attach a border which is too long as this causes a wavy edge to appear round the quilt.

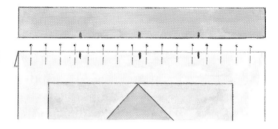

To avoid a wavy edge, ease the quilt top on to the border. Measure the finished quilt top down both the central length and the side lengths. If there is much discrepancy at the sides, take a measurement somewhere between the two and cut the borders to this size. Divide the borders and the body of the quilt into quarters and mark with pins. Matching these points carefully, pin border and quilt together using horizontal pins. Leave the pins in place, even if you tack, and then stitch the border to the quilt. Repeat the procedure across the width of the quilt.

MAKING A BIAS STRIP

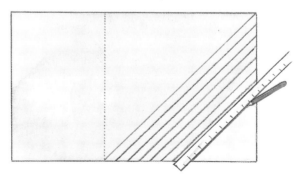

Fold the fabric so that the cut edge is parallel to the selvedge edge. The 45° angle on this triangle is the bias. Press the fold, trying not to stretch it out of shape, then use the fold as a guide to measure out and cut strips for Celtic and stained glass appliqué, bindings, pipings and rouleaux.

APPLYING BINDING

Pin binding on right side of the fabric, right sides facing and edges aligning. Tack and machine stitch in position with a 6mm (¼in) seam allowance. Turn the other edge of the binding on to the wrong side and slip stitch (page 148).

PIPING

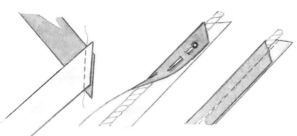

Cut lengths of bias strip 32mm (1¼in) wide and join them by placing two diagonal ends together and machine stitching with a 6mm (¼in) seam allowance. Press the seams open. Place pre-shrunk cotton piping cord along the centre of the strip, fold the strip over to enclose the cord and tack with a self coloured thread (it need not be pulled out later). Piping can also be machine stitched using a zip or piping foot close to the cord. Piping cord comes in several thicknesses, so select one suitable for your project, cutting the bias strips wider to accommodate thicker cord. Place the piping strip on the right side of the project, aligning raw edges. Tack or machine stitch in place, using the zip foot or a piping foot, close to the piping cord.

CELTIC BARS (BIAS PRESS BARS)

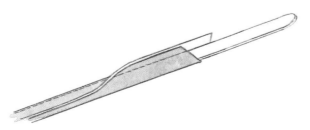

These are special metal or heat-resistant plastic strips bought in packets of three or four. Cut bias binding to fit one of the bars, according to manufacturers' instructions, then machine along the edge to make a tube. Insert the bar into the bias tube and press the seam allowance to one side, using the bar to form accurate folds. The seam allowance is hidden on the wrong side of the resulting strip as it is applied to a background fabric.

BIAS ROULEAUX

Very fine rouleaux can be made with thin silk or polyester fabric. Cut a bias strip 12mm (½in) wide. Use a polyester machine thread to stitch a tube, running the machine stitch off at an angle at the end of the strip to make a wide opening. Pull a long length of thread from the machine and cut. Thread a bodkin on to the thread, knotting it firmly in the eye. Pass the bodkin back through the tube, using damp fingers to help it on its way. Pull the bodkin through, gently but firmly, to turn the tube inside out. Practise this technique, but each time make the bias strip slightly narrower.

MAKING A CUSHION COVER

1 Measure the cushion pad, cut out the front and back pieces, adding an extra 4cm (1½in) across the back and 12mm (½in) all round for ease and seam allowances. Cut the back piece in half across the centre, turn under the cut edges 12mm (½in) and press in place. Pin the zip between these two edges, tack and machine stitch in position.
2 Check that the cushion front and back pieces are the same size, then open the zip slightly. Pin them together with right sides facing and machine stitch all round with a seam allowance of 6mm (¼in). Trim the corners, open the zip fully and turn right side out. Insert the cushion pad.

LACING FABRIC ROUND CARD

Lace fabric round card before framing. Use a strong thread which will not snap easily, such as buttonhole thread, linen carpet thread or very fine string.

1 Cut the card to the required size. Place the fabric right side up over the card, fold over the top and secure with pins pushed right into the edge of the cardboard. Repeat along the bottom. Keep the fabric grain straight.

2 Using a long thread, take long stitches between the two fabric edges, starting at the top left. When you have reached the bottom, remove the pins. Knot the thread securely at the starting point, then move downwards from stitch to stitch, tightening them as you go. Secure the thread end.

3 Repeat the pinning and lacing along the remaining two sides.

MAKING PRAIRIE POINTS

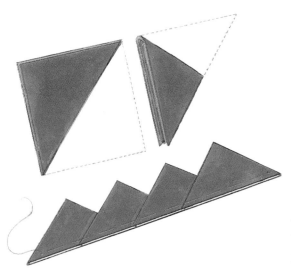

To make a prairie point, fold a small square of fabric diagonally in half, then fold diagonally again. The diagram shows how to arrange the prairie points in a strip. This technique is also known as a sawtooth edge.

MAKING SUFFOLK PUFFS

Cut a circle of fabric 10cm (4in) in diameter, turn a narrow hem round the edge and secure with a row of running stitches (page 147), beginning and ending with a length of thread. Gather up

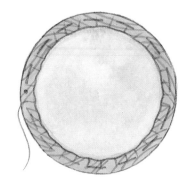

the running stitches and knot the thread ends together. Use your fingers to adjust the gathers to make an even circle. You can use any size of circle and insert a small piece of fabric inside the central gathers.

MAKING A TASSEL

You will need a skein of pearl cotton or coton à broder and a bead or small cotton ball. Wind lengths of embroidery thread about 40 times around a piece of card 12cm (4½in) long. Cut through the wound thread at one end and tie a piece of thread at the opposite end to hold the threads together, leaving the ends about 7cm (3in) long. Place a bead or cotton ball inside the lengths of thread, then bind a length of thread round just underneath the bead to hold it in place. Thread a tapestry needle with a 30cm (12in) length of thread and, beginning at the top of the bead, work rows of detached buttonhole stitch (page 149) to cover the bead. Finish off the thread, then trim the ends of the tassel.

Stitch library

QUILTING STITCHES

Whether working in the hand, or with any type of quilting frame, use both your hands when quilting. The finger beneath the quilt will ensure that each stitch pierces the backing correctly, Some people use their finger nail or finger tip for this purpose, but plastic guards can be purchased which save blisters. At first, the quilting process is very much trial and error but you will soon find the way which suits you. Some quilters like to give the quilting thread a little tug after every few stitches, others prefer a flatter effect.

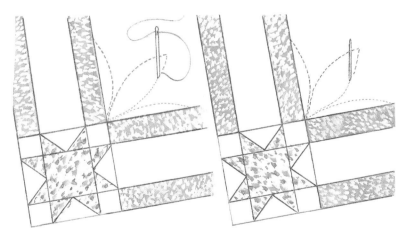

Stab stitch: The needle is passed from the top of the quilt to the hand beneath and then passed back. This method can give small stitches on the front of the quilt but the back is often untidy.

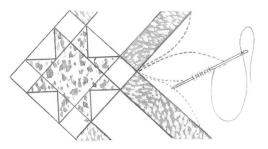

Running stitch: The most widely used method of working is to scoop the needle into the quilt, so the point touches a finger held underneath the quilt. Some quilters prefer to receive a tiny prick from the needle to ensure that it has gone through, others rely on a callous building up on their finger. When using a thimble, you can hear the scrape as the needle touches it. Several running stitches can be 'loaded' on to the needle or they can be worked one at a time.

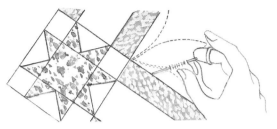

Rocking: A method of working running stitch by using a rocking movement to guide the needle in and out of the fabric. It can be worked by using the thumb as a guide to produce small stitches.

Whichever method of working you choose, be sure that each stitch goes right through to the back. Although some quilters take pride in making as many as 18 stitches to 2.5cm (1in), a more realistic ambition would be to work even stitches both back and front.

Begin by cutting a length of quilting thread about 36cm (14in) long. Run it through a cake of beeswax when the thread is unwaxed. Don't use a longer length of thread as it may fray either in the eye of the needle or during use. Make a knot at one end, then slide the needle into the quilt top about 2.5cm (1in) away from where you will be starting to stitch and bring the needle through at the correct point on the surface of the fabric. Tug the knot so that it pops through below the surface and is lost in the wadding. Work a small back stitch (page 149) then carry on with your quilting stitch until there is about 6cm (2½in) of thread left. Tie a knot and run it down the thread. Make the last stitch and tug the knot through the fabric. Work a small back stitch to finish, bringing the thread out about 2.5cm (1in) away and cutting off the end carefully. Alternatively, lose the end of the thread in a handy seam. Areas of over 10cm (4in) width or length should not be left unquilted as the wadding might tear during washing.

SEWING STITCHES

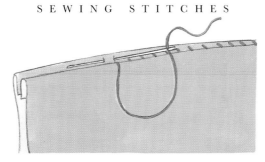

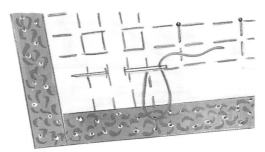

Ladder stitch: Originally a tailoring stitch, ladder stitch is useful for making invisible joins between the folded edges of two pieces of fabric. Run the needle along one fold and bring it out, passing it through the other fold, directly opposite the exit hole. This method can also be used to join checks, stripes and patterned fabrics.

Tacking: Worked in the same way as running stitch (above), but use a long needle and make the stitches larger.

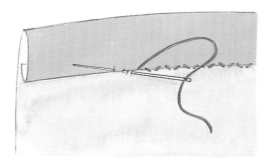

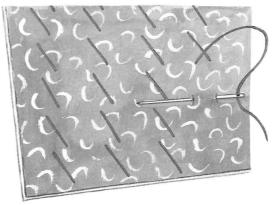

Slip stitch: Slip stitch is used for securing the folded edge of binding and hems. Run the needle along the fold, bring it out and take a stitch directly opposite. Bring out the needle so that it runs again inside the fold. The tiny stitches should be straight, not sloping. The smaller the stitch, the less thread is seen. In appliqué, match the thread to the motif, not the background.

Diagonal tacking: Used to secure layers of fabric and wadding together instead of grid tacking. Work the stitches in a vertical direction towards your body, as shown.

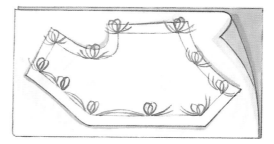

Oversewing: Used to join the patches in 'English' method patchwork from the wrong side. Work oversewing over the edge of the folds to be joined, with the needle towards you. The stitches should be small and straight and almost invisible from the right side.

Tailors' tacks: A stitch used to mark a point or line on a piece of fabric. Tailor's tacks are also used to mark both sides of a double layer of fabric accurately. Work a double horizontal stitch, leaving loops of thread on the top fabric, then 'float' the thread along the top of the fabric before working another double stitch. After all the tailors' tacks have been worked, cut the thread loops and the 'float' between very carefully. Then part the two layers of fabric and snip the stitches between.

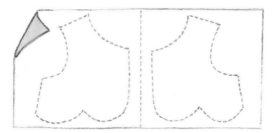

Trace tack: This is a guide line of running stitches (page 147) used to show the stitching line on a piece of fabric. It is used for patterns without a seam allowance, in clothing and also to work guide lines when marking up quilt designs.

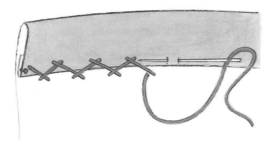

Herringbone stitch: Used for joining wadding and for closing the gap in backing fabric after a shape has been stuffed. When using this stitch to join wadding, make sure the edges are butted together, then work the herringbone across the join. Working from left to right, bring the needle through the fabric along the lower edge, then make a short stitch from right to left along the top edge. Make a second stitch along the lower edge and repeat.

DECORATIVE
STITCHES

Chain stitch: Work chain stitch downwards by making a series of loops of identical size. Anchor the last loop with a small straight stitch.

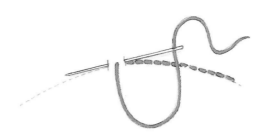

Back stitch: Work back stitch from left to right, making small, regular stitches that look like machine stitching. Work the stitches forwards and backwards along the line.

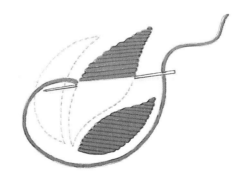

Satin stitch: Bring the needle through at the edge of the shape to be filled, carry the thread across the shape, then return it beneath the fabric close to the point where it emerged. Work the stitches closely together so the fabric is covered.

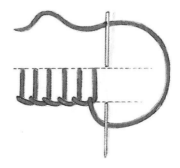

Detached buttonhole stitch: Work a row of buttonhole stitches round the top of the tassel or at the top of the shape being filled. Work subsequent rows of buttonhole stitch through the loops on the previous row. Make a buttonhole loop by stranding the thread several times to make a loop shape, then cover the loop with closely worked buttonhole stitches.

L O O K I N G   A F T E R   Y O U R
Q U I L T

CLEANING QUILTS

Unless your fabric has been pre-washed (page 66), always test to see if the dyes from strongly coloured areas are going to run before attempting to wash a quilt. Dampen the patch and blot with a piece of white cotton cloth. Examine the cloth carefully for loose dye.

Quilts can be washed in a large washing machine on the delicate fabrics cycle if you are confident that the colours will not run. However, once the machine has started you have very little control over events! It is generally safer to wait for a warm day and use a bath. Two pairs of hands are an asset during the washing process. Use a gentle washing powder without bleach or brighteners and dissolve it in warm water. Fold the quilt to fit the bath, immerse it in the water, gently pat and squeeze, then let the water run out of the bath.

Work as quickly as you can, not allowing the quilt to soak, which gives dyes the chance to run. Rinse several times in cool water. After the last rinse, press the quilt against the sides of the bath then lift it and allow the water to run out for a few moments.

The wet quilt will be heavy and if you can transport it to the garden in a baby bath, so much the better – or put it in a large plastic bag. Gently lay the quilt out on old towels or sheets, blot with another towel and leave to dry out of direct sunlight, turning it over from time to time. Rig up two parallel, firmly fixed, clothes lines and hang the quilt over these when partially dry. Do not press.

Wallhangings should, from time to time, be taken down from the wall and shaken gently, then vacuumed carefully with a piece of net fastened over the cleaner's nozzle. Depending on the fabric which has been used, wallhangings may be washed in the same way as a quilt. When dry cleaning quilting, use a reliable firm and make sure *stress* that the quilt should not be pressed. Dry cleaning is not recommended for baby wear or cot quilts as the cleaning agent produces strong fumes.

STORING QUILTS

Do not store quilts wrapped in polythene as the plastic attracts dirt both inside and out. Fabric needs to breathe and air will prevent mildew from forming, so it is better to make a large calico bag for your quilt with an overlap closure like a pillowcase. Take out the quilt from time to time and refold it to help prevent permanent crease marks. When storing a quilt rolled round a carpet or similar cardboard tube, cover the tube in acid-free tissue and roll the quilt round it with the right side to the outside, which will help prevent creasing. Wrap in tissue and make a calico tube bag. Don't forget to label your bags.

SENDING QUILTS TO EXHIBITIONS

Whenever possible, try to deliver and collect your quilt from exhibitions yourself. However, if you are sending one through the post or by carrier, be sure that insurance to cover the quilt's value is included in the cost. Place wadding off-cuts or bubble wrap inside the folded quilt, wrap in white tissue paper then seal in polythene. Tubular fabric delivery bags fit well. Post or send parcels at the beginning of the week, so they don't sit around in storage over the weekend and, if possible, ask the exhibition organisers to open up the polythene as soon as convenient.

SLEEVES FOR HANGING QUILTS

The majority of fabric dyes will not withstand strong sunlight without fading for more than a few hours. When selecting a position for a wallhanging, take this fact into account. This also applies to quilts on the window side of the bed. However, positioning a hanging or quilt away from direct light will slow the fading process down.

When sending a quilt to an exhibition or competition, try to hang your quilt before sending it off, just to check how it behaves. Most exhibition organisers specify a 10cm (4in) sleeve (a strip of fabric sewn on the wrong side of the quilt which accommodates a rod or batten for hanging the quilt on a wall). The sleeve can be attached in a variety of ways. The top edge can be incorporated into the quilt binding as it is slip stitched (page 148) in place. The bottom edge of the sleeve is then slip stitched on to the back of

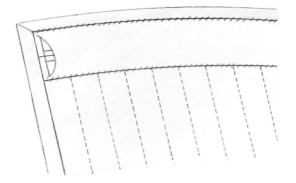

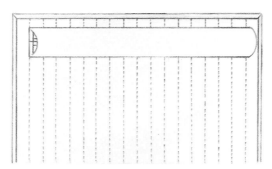

Glossary

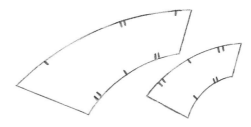

the quilt, with care, so that the stitches do not go right through to the front. Alternatively, use a tube of fabric. Press the tube flat, making sure that the seam will be concealed when it is slip stitched on to the quilt back.

You may like to attach a second sleeve to the lower edge of the quilt. Slot a piece of varnished batten into the sleeve to assist the hang of the quilt. Lengths of lead curtain weights can also be sewn into the hem.

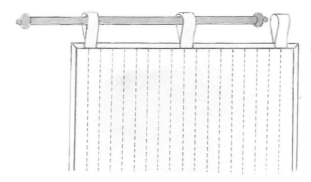

You can attach a series of fabric loops along the top edge of a hanging. Slot through a length of flat, varnished wood with holes drilled at either end for hanging. The wood should be cut just short of the sides of the hanging. A length of flat wood holds the hanging closer to the wall than a round pole.

Balance marks: Dressmaking marks used to align curved edges correctly before stitching a seam.

Clipping curves: Snip into the seam allowance along curves before stitching to assist the stretch and after stitching curved seams will lie flat. Take care not to cut into the stitching.

Drafted design: A full-size quilting design drawn out onto dressmaker's pattern paper.

Finger press: Pressing a seam flat between fingers when to press with an iron would not be appropriate.

Loft: refers to the height of the wadding when it has been quilted.

On point: means that the square is turned to form a diamond. The rows of blocks run diagonally from corner to corner.

Pinch mark or finger crease: A quick method to mark a measurement without using pins or pencil. Press the fabric firmly between thumb and forefinger.

Reef knot: A non-slip knot tied by passing the thread ends right over left, then left over right.

Rouleau: A narrow tube made from fabric, always cut on the bias.

The set: refers to the way patchwork blocks are arranged within a quilt.

Template: A shape cut from card or plastic which is laid on the fabric then drawn round with a pencil prior to cutting out. A template may or may not have the seam allowance added, so always check this before cutting.

Trimming or clipping corners: Trim off surplus fabric diagonally from the seam allowance after corners have been stitched to reduce bulk. This is particularly important when making a cushion cover or other rectangular item that will be turned to the right side after stitching.

Useful Addresses

Shops selling to personal callers only

UK

Borovicks, 16 Berwick Street, London W1V 4HP (pure silk and glitzy fabric)

Chattels, 53 Chalk Farm Road, London NW1 8AN (quilts and materials)

Maple Textiles, 188–190 Maple Road, Penge, London SE20 8HT (textile craft supplies)

Patchworks and Quilts, 9 West Place, Wimbledon, London SW19 4UH (quilts and materials)

The Stitchery, 6 Finkle Street, Richmond, N Yorks, DL10 4QA (threads)

CANADA

Quilter's Fancy, 2877 Bloor Street West, Toronto, ON M8X 1B3 (books and materials)

NEW ZEALAND

Bennetts Bookshop, 38–42 Broadway, PO Box 138, Palmerston North

SOUTH AFRICA

Daih's Materials, Grootfontein Centre, Sasolburg, Transvaal

Roodeport Country Patchwork, Ruimsig, 383 Stallion Road, Transvaal

The Craft Gallery, PO Box 2062, Beacon Bay, East London, Cape Province

Kalicoscope, PO Box 4206, Durban 4000

Lavender Blue, The Cottles, 4th Avenue, Parkhurst, Johannesburg

Les Designs, 21 Orchards Road, Orchards, Johannesburg (kits, books and franchise teacher network)

Pickles and Patchwork, Pinelands, Cape Town

Pied Piper, Port Elizabeth, Cape Province

Quilters' Companion, Margaret le Roux, PO Box 1447, Wandsbeck 3631, Natal (quilting rulers and squares)

Stitch Talk, Verwoerdburgstad, Transvaal

Shops selling to personal callers and mail order service

UK

The Country Store (formerly Pioneer Patches), 68 Westbourne Road, Marsh, Huddersfield, W Yorks

Crimple Craft, 1 Freemans Way, Forest Lane, Wetherby Road, Harrogate, Yorks, HG3 1RW

Green Hill, 27 Bell Street, Romsey, Hants, SO51 8GY

Piecemakers, 13 Manor Green Road, Epsom, Surrey, KT19 8RA (large range of fabric)

The Quilt Room, 20 West Street, Dorking, Surrey, RH4 1BL (fabric, quilting supplies including freezer paper)

Mail order only

UK

Craft Publications, Marsh Mills, Luck Lane, Huddersfield, W Yorks, HD3 4AB (craft books)

Leicester Laminating Services, 71 Westfield Road, Weston Park, Leics LE3 6HU (plastic graph and template material)

Magpie Patchworks, 37 Palfrey Road, Northbourne, Bournemouth, Dorset, BH10 6DN (fabric)

HW Peel & Co Ltd, Chartwell House, 1c Lyon Way, Rockware Estate, Greenford, Middlesex, UB6 0BN (Chartwell graph and isometric paper)

Quilt Basics, 2 Meades Lane, Chesham, Bucks, HP5 1ND (reducing glass)

Silken Strands, 33 Linksway, Gatley, Cheadle, Cheshire, SK8 4LA (beads and embroidery threads)

Strawberry Fayre, Chagford, Devon, TQ13 8EN (fabric including Amish range)

Threadbare Embroidery Requisites, Glenfield Park, Glenfield Road, Nelson, Lancs, BB9 8AR (unusual embroidery materials)

Threadbear Supplies, 11 Northway, Deanshanger, Milton Keynes, MK19 6NF (wadding)

Associations and guilds

UK

National Patchwork Association, PO Box 300, Hethersett, Norwich, Norfolk, NR9 3DB tel: 0603 812259

The Quilters' Guild, Unit OP66, Dean Clough, Halifax, W Yorks, HX3 5AX tel: 0422 347669 (Members receive a quarterly full-colour magazine.

Both of the above associations will put individuals in touch with local quilting groups)
Patchwork Guild of Northern Ireland, c/o Irene MacWilliam, 67 Drumbeg Road, Dunmurry, Belfast, Northern Ireland BT17 9LE

EUROPE
Dansk Patchwork Forening, c/o Jytte Rendboe, H Jallesegade 46, DK-5260 Odense S, Denmark
Irish Patchwork Society, PO Box 45, Blackrock, County Dublin, Ireland
Association Francaise du Patchwork, Boite Postale 100-16, F75763 Paris Cedex 16K, France
Patchwork Gilde, c/o Ingeborg Thormann, Bungerweg 6A, D-2000 Hamburg-52, Germany
Swiss Patchwork Association, c/o Isabel Schneider, 4 Chemin des Jardillets, CH-2068 Hauterive, Switzerland

SOUTH AFRICA
South African Quilt Teachers' Association, 5 Protea Close, Pinelands 7405

AUSTRALIA AND NEW ZEALAND
Alice Springs Quilting Group, PO Box 3301, Alice Springs, NT 5750
Australian Quilters' Association, PO Box 497, Hawthorn, Vic 3122
Canberra Quilters Inc, PO Box 29, Jamison Centre, ACT 2614
Darwin Patchworkers and Quilters, PO Box 518, Humpty Doo, NT 5791
2Q-Queensland Quilters, GPO Box 2841, Brisbane, Qld 4001
The Quilters' Guild Inc, PO Box 654, Neutral Bay, NSW 2089
Quilters' Guild of South Australia Inc, PO Box 993, Norwood, SA 5067
Tasmanian Quilting Guild, PO Box 1217, Gravelly Beach, Tas 7251
The Western Australian Quilters' Association Inc, PO Box 188, Subiaco, WA 6008
Auckland Patchwork and Quilters' Guild, 51 Third Avenue, Kingsland, Auckland 3
E Herbert, Canterbury Patchwork and Quilters' Guild, 5 Woodford Terrace, Christchurch 5
National Patchwork and Quilting Symposium Inc, PO Box 11-051, Wellington
Mrs A Pibal, Editor, Capital Quilters, 52 Kanni Street, Wainuimati
Dunedin Patchwork Guild, PO Box 5664, Dunedin Quilt Symposium, PO Box 11/051, Wellington

Magazines

UK
Patchwork & Quilting, 1 Highfield Close, Malvern Link, Worcs, WR14 1SH tel: 0684 573966

AUSTRALIA
Down Under Quilts, PO Box 619, Beenleigh, Qld 4207

NEW ZEALAND
New Zealand Quilter, PO Box 9202, Wellington

UK Exhibition organisers

The Great British Quilt Festival, 13 Stourton Road, Ainsdale, Southport, Merseyside, PR8 3LP tel: 0704 737424
National Patchwork Championships, PO Box 300, Hethersett, Norwich, Norfolk, NR9 3DB tel: 0603 812259
Quilts UK, 1 Highfield Close, Malvern Link, Worcs, WR14 1SH tel: 0684 573966

UK Commissions

Quilt Art, c/o Deirdre Amsden, 38a Limehouse Cut, 46 Morris Road, Poplar, London E14 6NQ
The Quilter's Guild, Unit OP66, Dean Clough, Halifax, W Yorks, HX3 5AX tel: 0422 347669

UK Galleries displaying and selling quilts

The Crane Gallery, 171a Sloane Street, London SW1X 9QG
Museum Quilts, 3rd Floor, 254-258 Goswell Road, London EC1V 7EB

UK Galleries and museums with quilt collections

The American Museum in Britain, Claverton Manor, Bath, Avon, BA2 7BD tel: 0225 60503
Beamish North of England Open Air Museum, Beamish, Stanley, County Durham, DH9 0RG tel: 0207 231811
The Bowes Museum, Barnard Castle, County Durham, DL12 8NP tel: 0833 37139
Carlisle Museum & Art Gallery, Tullie House, Castle Street, Carlisle, CA3 8TP tel: 0228 34781 (contact Keeper of Fine Art for an appointment to view)

The Castle Museum, Tower Street, York, YO1 1RY tel: 0904 53611 (contact Keeper of Textiles for appointment to view)

Cheltenham Art Gallery and Museums, 40 Clarence Street, Cheltenham, Glos, GL50 3NX tel: 0242 37431 (contact Assistant Keeper of Applied Arts for appointment to view)

Gawthorpe Hall, Padiham, Nr Burnley, Lancs, BB12 8UA tel: 0282 78511 (quilts from Rachel K Shuttleworth collection available for personal study by arrangement with the Curator)

Levens Hall, Kendal, Cumbria, LA8 0PB tel: 0448 60321

Manx Museum and National Trust, Douglas, Isle of Man tel: 0624 675522 (contact Curator for an appointment to view)

Museum of English Native Art, The Countess of Huntingdon Chapel, The Vineyard Paragon, Bath, Avon tel: 0225 446020

Museum of Lakeland Life and Industry, Abbot Hall, Kendal, Cumbria, LA9 5AL tel: 0539 22464

Museum of Mankind, 6 Burlington Gardens, London W1X 2EX

Royal Scottish Museum, Chambers Street, Edinburgh, EH1 1JF tel: 031 225 7534

Shipley Art Gallery, Prince Consort Road, Gateshead, Tyne and Wear, NE8 4JB tel: 091 477 1495 (information service available on quilts and quilting)

Strangers' Hall Museum, Charing Cross, Norwich, Norfolk, NR2 4AL tel: 0603 611277 (contact Curator for an appointment to view)

Ulster Folk and Transport Museum, Cultra Manor, Holywood, County Down, BT18 0EU tel 023 175411

Victoria and Albert Museum, Cromwell Road, South Kensington, London SW7 2RL tel: 071 589 6371

Welsh Folk Museum, St Fagans, Cardiff, CF5 6XB tel: 0222 569441

Further Reading

Adachi, Fumie: Japanese Design Motifs *(Dover) 1972*

Bain, George: Celtic Art: The Method of Construction *(Constable)*

Barker, Vicki and Bird, Tessa: The Fine Art of Quilting *(Studio Vista) 1990*

Colby, Averil: Patchwork *(Batsford) 1958*

Colby, Averil: Quilting *(Batsford) 1983*

Jones, Owen: The Grammar of Ornament *(Omega Press) 1986*

McDowell, Ruth B: Pattern on Pattern *(The Quilt Digest Press) 1991*

Osler, Dorothy: Traditional British Quilts *(Batsford) 1987*

Osler, Dorothy: Quilting *(Merehurst) 1991*

Turpin-Delport, Lesley: A Creative Guide to Patchwork and Appliqué *(New Holland) 1988*

Turpin-Delport, Lesley: The Complete Book of Appliqué and Patchwork *(New Holland) 1986*

Turpin-Delport, Lesley: Quilts and Quilting: A Creative Guide *(New Holland) 1991*

Travis, Dinah: The Sampler Quilt Workbook *(Batsford) 1990*

Wade, David: Geometric Patterns & Borders *(Wildwood House, London) 1982*

Walker, Michelle: The Complete Book of Quiltmaking *(Windward/Frances Lincoln) 1989*

Wien, Carol Anne: The Great American Log Cabin Book *(Dutton) 1990*

Index

Acknowledgements

The author would like to thank the following:
Robert for hours of calm and practical help
Hugo Moss for his help with the computer design on page 25
Carole Hart for sewing 'Wish You Were Here', page 132
Pat Taylor for quilting and making the Sashiko jacket on page 126
Tina Newholm for quilting the Amish quilt on page 70, the playmat
on page 118 and the silk cushion on page 94
Bunny Binstead for the 'Celtic Bag' tassel, page 79
Jenni Dobson for quilting 'One O'Clock Jump', page 114
Trudi Billingsley for her 'Basque Belt', page 76
Sheila Yale for designing and making 'A Colourful Story' page 90
Beckenham Quilters for making 'Huge Curves', page 100
Jan Eaton for editing the book and holding my hand
Steve Tanner for his skilful photography

Maple Textiles for giving me the run of their shop and providing
supplies from every department
The Crane Gallery for the loan of several slides
The Quilt Room for generously supplying the fabric for 'Huge Curves'
P & B Textiles for supplying fabric
Piecemakers for supplying materials
Strawberry Fayre for supplying fabric from their beautiful Amish range
Leicester Laminating Services for template plastic
Chartwell for isometric and graph paper
PlantCare II, 96–98 Highbury Park, London N5 2XE Tel: 071 226 6000
for the branches and pots on page 87

Plus: Pierrette Hoare, Kathleen Hodgson, Joan Jeffard,
Jean Lendon, Mary Trim, The Country Store, Patchworks
and Quilts, Coats Patons Crafts, The Stitchery

Special Photography Steve Tanner: pp. 1, 2–3, 5, 9, 10–11, 13–14, 16–17,
18–19, 21, 22–23, 24, 26–29, 31–33, 36–38, 42–43, 47–49, 50–52, 54–55,
58–59, 60, 62, 65–69, 71, 73, 75–77, 79, 82–83, 87, 91–92, 94–95, 97,
101–102, 105, 108–109, 115–116, 119–120, 122–123, 126–127,
131–133, 135–136, 137, 152–153.
Illustrations: Terry Evans pp. 74–75, 80–81 (top), 84–85, 86, 98–99 (left top &
bottom), 100, 102, 104, 106 (left top & bottom), 112–113 (left top & bottom),
128, 134, 139, 141–149, 151 and Stephen Dew pp. 72, 78, 81, 88–89, 93, 96,
99 (right), 103, 106 (right)–107, 111, 113 (right), 117, 121, 124, 125, 129, 130.